P9-CQO-317

SUCCULENTS

The Ultimate Guide to
Choosing, Designing, and Growing
200 Easy-Care Plants

—

By ROBIN STOCKWELL

with
Kathleen Norris Brenzel

Oxmoor
House.

Published by Oxmoor House, an imprint of
Time Inc. Books
225 Liberty Street, New York, NY 10281

EDITORS Kathleen N. Brenzel, Betty Wong
CREATIVE DIRECTOR Maili Holiman
DESIGNER Christy Sheppard Knell
PRODUCTION MANAGER Linda M. Bouchard
PHOTO EDITOR Linda Lamb Peters
COPY EDITOR Judith Dunham
IMAGING SPECIALISTS Kimberley Navabpour,
E. Spencer Toy
PROJECT EDITOR Melissa Brown
ASSISTANT PRODUCTION MANAGER Lauren Moriarty
PROOFREADER Denise Griffiths
INDEXER Ken DellaPenta

For additional credits, see page 282.

ISBN-13: 978-0-8487-4947-7

Library of Congress Control Number: 2016944980

Printed in the United States of America

10 9 8 7 6 5 4 3 2 1

First Printing 2017

Time Inc. Books products may be purchased for
business or promotional use. For information on bulk
purchases, please contact Christi Crowley in the
Special Sales Department at (845) 895-9858.

We welcome your comments and suggestions about
Time Inc. Books.
Please write to us at:
Time Inc. Books
Attention: Book Editors
P.O. Box 62310
Tampa, Florida 33662-2310

———

To each of my children, who have
supported me in a quest that involved sacrifice
and at times did not make a lot of sense.
To my wife, a dedicated nurse, who has always
had the back of this small businessman,
nurseryman, and succulent plant grower—and
throughout the writing of this book.

———

16
INSPIRATIONS

Find fabulous design ideas to inspire your own succulent garden.

A display garden at Flora Grubb nursery in San Francisco.

FOREWORD

LONG BEFORE MY GARDEN STORE became a gathering place for design-driven gardeners and landscape professionals, I was just a gal from Texas who had moved to California and, in 2001, opened a small nursery and store in San Francisco with a partner. My vision was to create plant displays that would encourage shoppers to design beautiful landscapes requiring minimal water and chemicals. But I wasn't exactly sure how to make that happen.

Then I met Robin Stockwell. The first time I visited his nursery, Succulent Gardens, a light went on for me as a nurserywoman and as a designer. Seeing all his plants together in the greenhouses, I thought, "These plants belong in gardens." I began to stock my store with them.

Since then, Robin has been more than a wholesale plant supplier to me: He has become an inspiration and mentor, generously sharing his experience with plants and retailing, and helping me to clarify my vision for what Flora Grubb Gardens could become. He encouraged me to push toward a design-focused nursery and not to worry about folks who thought our plants should be priced like those at big box stores. The plants Robin was growing in the early days of my nursery were unique and unrivaled. So much of what Flora Grubb Gardens became is because, behind the scenes, Robin was providing such gorgeous plants for all our creations.

In fact, I was embarrassed by just how much of Robin's work was credited to me. Robin and I hung a vertical garden in my nursery that he had planted and grown. Images of that planting went viral, attracting tons of attention and new visitors to my store. One day I told him, "My name is all over your work! I get the credit for simply selling what you created." Although I don't recall his exact reply, Robin's response was good-humored and generous, and I was deeply touched.

In this book, we see Robin's ideas come to life in stunning images of gardens, bouquets, and more. We also learn more about Robin. He is a man who navigates with his heart. He conducts business, grows plants, and mentors newbies like me in the world of landscapes with kindness, enthusiasm, and a guiding sense of wonder for the natural world. I am so grateful to have benefited from my years of friendship with him, and so delighted that he has created this book—a gift to garden lovers everywhere.

—Flora Grubb
Owner, Flora Grubb Gardens, San Francisco

SUNSET, THE SURFER, AND SUCCULENTS

"SUCCULENTS—ECCENTRIC, VARIED, ALWAYS INTERESTING—have moved in and out of Western gardens on the tide of public fancy. Now they are coming back into favor again, and this time it looks like something more than a temporary infatuation."

So predicted the June 1954 issue of *Sunset* magazine in an article that went on to tout amazing facts about succulents. That they are found in every part of the world where plants have difficulty getting and holding water—in the deserts of North and South America, Africa, and Mexico; in the high mountains of the Arctic and Antarctic regions where cold makes absorption of moisture difficult; in rocky or sandy soils where water quickly evaporates or drains away; or in brackish ground where the high concentration of salt hinders the plants' absorption of water. That they have built-in defenses such as fleshy, waxy, or fuzzy leaves for holding water—developed over millions of years as they struggled in barren places for life-giving moisture. (The word *succulent* is derived from the Latin *suculentus*, meaning "juicy or fleshy.") And that, by nature, succulents are perhaps the most efficiently designed of all plants for easy propagation. They not only reproduce by seed but, in many species, can multiply spontaneously by fallen leaves, branches, or shoots. Because they carry their own moisture, they can quickly root on dry ground. And they're made for growing in containers. Tolerance for drought and neglect enables them to survive lapses in care that could be fatal to other patio container plants—a major plus in warm climates.

Still, these remarkable plants continued to grow quietly in collectors' backyards—in dish gardens, in parking strips, in pocket-size beds edging patios—with only occasional upticks in popularity after that *Sunset* article appeared. Serious droughts during the 1970s provided further incentive for some gardeners to try growing succulents, even the rocklike *Lithops*, which they laughingly referred to as "doorknob plants." And after devastating wildfires destroyed gardens in arid parts of the West, homeowners began to appreciate the way that succulents survived while other plants perished.

Robin Stockwell at Carmel shop, 1984.

The Surfer

In the early 1980s, a surfer dude named Robin Stockwell began to launch these plants into the spotlight to stay. Robin, who had grown up near Half Moon Bay, California, and surfed the waves there, had just opened a small shop in Carmel where *Sunset* editors discovered him planting his succulent pictures to frame and sell for displaying on walls. We published an article about his succulent bouquets in 1981 and another on his living pictures in 1984. More articles touting his plants would follow.

This guy, I decided the moment I met him, thinks BIG. His enthusiasm for succulents is infectious. And he's game to try any project that shows off his gorgeous plants in a fresh way, no matter how large or daunting. Robin began to collaborate with us on a variety of projects, arriving at our Northern California campus in his truck laden with plants. Among his creations for us: beach-themed succulent pots to display outside a *Sunset* Idea House; a rockery in our test garden with rosettes blooming among angular boulders; and a border of striking magenta-flowered *Calandrinia* tucked among chocolate-hued *Aeonium* rosettes. For a *Sunset* display garden at the San Francisco Flower and Garden Show, we teamed Robin

A succulent garden at San Francisco International Airport.

with ornamental grass expert John Greenlee, tropical plants expert and garden designer Davis Dalbok of Living Green Design, and Mike Boss of Rock & Rose Landscapes, to create a series of lush gardens that flowed into one another. That display garden was a highlight of the show!

As Robin gradually expanded his business to become one of the largest wholesale providers of succulents on the West Coast, his nursery—which produced and displayed some 400 varieties and well over 100,000 plants in 2-inch pots to whoppers in 24-inch boxes—became a mecca for landscape professionals, hobbyists, home gardeners, and college horticulture students.

To share his succulent wisdom, Robin spoke at garden club events and garden shows, and invited kids from nearby schools to attend dish garden classes at Succulent Gardens Nursery. After touring the nursery, the kids would grab pots and plant them, then depart, hugging their pots close. "I did everything I could to promote succulent plants," Robin told me.

The Succulent World

At the same time, succulents were turning up in public places—atop the south promontory of the J. Paul Getty Center in Los Angeles, in boulevard medians in San Francisco, in borders at chic beachside hotels in Southern California, and in window boxes outside boutiques in Portland, Oregon. They decorated restaurant walls near San Diego and patios at the San Francisco International Airport. And they filled alpine troughs at the Denver Botanic Gardens and special sections at Seattle nurseries. Women started adorning hatbands with tiny live rosettes, pals formed succulent fan clubs, and florists began specializing in succulent arrangements. Succulent cafes popped up where visitors could sip lattes surrounded by plants they could later purchase.

In September 2010, Robin held his first Succulent Extravaganza, an annual, weekend long open house at Succulent Gardens Nursery that attracted some 1,500 visitors per year. They came to learn from expert speakers about growing these plants and to swap stories with other succulent aficionados over tacos and barbecue fare. They wandered among display gardens, like the big succulent "wave"—rearing up and appearing ready to break—that landscape architect Steve Sutherland built by studding mounded earth with blue and green succulents to celebrate Robin's love of surfing. And they came to buy plants.

Now, succulents have taken over the Internet and social media as well, with websites such as Debra Lee Baldwin's (with more than 2 million page views), to feed the hunger for design ideas and succulent-related news. Fans post images of their latest creations on Instagram and Pinterest, and blog about them. Succulent Fanatics, a Facebook group founded by San Jose Master Gardener Laura Balaoro, has members living as far away as South America and who exchange ideas online and meet at succulent events.

But without plant material, there would be no surge in succulent popularity. "I'm a grower with vision," Robin told me. "I truly wanted people to see these plants in a different light than they had in the past. I pushed the limit, taking succulents to a new level. My softer, more colorful designs got people excited and set them off on their own journeys of creativity. That's what catapulted succulents onto the world's horticultural stage."

I often tell people that Robin knows more about succulents than just about anyone. That is why I'm delighted that, with this book, he is passing along all that he has learned about these plants over the years. Thanks to Robin Stockwell, gorgeous succulents are now more available to us all, to stoke our creative fires.

—Kathleen N. Brenzel
Garden Editor Emeritus, *Sunset* magazine

SUCCULENTS:
A GROWER'S PERSPECTIVE

MY FIRST EXPOSURE TO SUCCULENTS came in the spring of 1973, while driving to Monterey with my college buddy, Gerry Moran. Intrigued by a sign pointing to Mulligan Hill Cactus, near Castroville, we pulled off the main highway and followed a dusty road up to the hillside farm in the middle of the artichoke fields. The eclectic collection of cactus we found there lay scattered on the ground beside the ranch foreman's house. The plants were not labeled; they grew in milk cartons and cans of all shapes and sizes, from tuna and soup cans to bean and beer cans. That didn't appear to phase the plants: They were all covered with bright flowers of red, yellow, orange, white, and more. Great big flowers topped columnar *Trichocereus*, and garlands of tiny flowers crowned *Mammillaria* cactus. I was captivated. Plants use people, wrote Michael Pollan in *The Botany of Desire*. And I believe that succulents latched onto me at that moment, in that cactus patch, and chose me to be their lifetime spokesman. I bought the whole lot on the spot and sold them, along with a few succulents, at a houseplant nursery that Gerry and I later started to supply Bay Area plant shops.

Over time, I learned that all cactus are succulents, but not all succulents are cactus. And I got to know the noncactus succulents as well, including agaves, aloes, aeoniums, echeverias, sempervivums, and sedums. I found them fascinating, especially their colorful foliage, their varied textures, their diversity and versatility. I began to see the different varieties as components of a palette, which I could use to create beautiful gardens.

After a stint in the houseplant business, in the mid-1970s I went out on my own, focusing totally on succulents. My goal was to create a successful product line that would sell. In order to get buyers' attention, though, I needed to become a showman. I had to convince these experts that succulents are just as pretty and possibly even more useful than other plants. So I produced a line of assorted succulents in 2-inch, 4-inch, and 6-inch pots, and then organized them attractively, by color and shape, on trays. I visited nurseries to show off my striking selections. The plant buyers, I discovered, had never seen succulents presented in such a colorful way. Slowly, their orders began to trickle in. Therein lies the great secret of

Me in my element, among succulents at the beach! Succulents allow me the freedom to go backpacking and surfing whenever I want, even for weeks at a time.

"THE GLOBE"

A project for the 2012 San Francisco Flower and Garden Show, this 10-foot sphere was planted with 20,000 succulents. To top it off, the globe rotated!

designing with succulents: If you present them well, you will show off their unique beauty to the fullest.

By 1979, I had produced the product line I envisioned, and my ideas about succulents had evolved. I learned how efficient these plants are at using water and nutrients, and how versatile they are in landscaping and container gardening. I experimented with cuttings in bouquets, working with researchers at the University of California at Davis to test them for "vase life" (which can be months long!). I also discovered how underutilized these incredible plants were in landscaping at that time, and how misunderstood they were by the professionals and by home gardeners. The demand for great quantities of these plants was still low. So I closed my wholesale operation and opened a small retail store in Carmel, California, to sell succulents in containers along with garden decor.

To replenish my supplies for the store, in 2003 I decided to grow my own plants again. I found a defunct carnation nursery in Castroville and rented a portion of it. Then I visited my old grower friends and collected mother stock. Gradually I grew the nursery. Within a couple of years, my plants were in a few retail nurseries in Northern California, and many customers, both wholesale and retail, began coming to my nursery.

But it took a series of changes in gardening styles to finally boost the demand for my plants. After severe droughts devastated gardens in the western United States, homeowners began removing thirsty lawns and replacing them with water-wise plants. At the same time, with smaller gardens becoming the new norm, rooftop gardening was coming into vogue, followed by the rising popularity of "vertical gardening." Landscape architects and designers began to use these plants in very creative ways. I started experimenting with elaborate vertical murals.

In 2005, I met two extraordinarily creative landscape designers, Sean Stout and James Pettigrew of Organic Mechanics. Over the next several years, I worked with them on several landscape projects for the annual San Francisco Flower and Garden Show—my plants, their talents. Many fabulous creations followed. Together, we proved that you really can grow succulents almost anywhere, on big canvases of any size or shape!

I sold my Succulent Gardens business in 2014. Growing succulents has been an incredible journey, one that I continue today in my own backyard. Succulents, I've discovered, are the true conservationists of the plant world—easy, undemanding of resources, water-thrifty. They make sense for gardens now, and for the future.

About This Book

As a grower, I have learned that gardeners often choose specific plants after seeing them used beautifully in someone else's garden, or in a pretty bouquet somewhere. So I have organized this book starting with Inspirations (page 16), which shows ideas from 22 gardens that use succulents creatively in all kinds of spaces, from narrow side yards to rooftops. Look to Easy Projects (page 126) for interesting new ideas on bringing succulents indoors; just follow my "recipes" to show off succulents in vases, containers, on birdhouses, and more. Once inspired, turn to My Favorite Plants (page 182), which profiles 203 kinds. If you're looking for a plant with a special job to do in your garden, first check out the Succulent Selection Guide on pages 184 and 185; it lists the best succulents to use as groundcovers, hedges, edgings, and more. Otherwise, browse through that chapter's many images, and select plants by the colors and forms you love, each accompanied by detailed information, such as how big it grows, when it blooms, plus exposure and water needs. Finally, in Planting and Care (page 246), you will find tips on succulent shopping (choose healthy plants), planting (in good soil!), plus watering, feeding, and caring for them.

If you have never grown succulents, this book will inspire and guide you. If you consider yourself a seasoned pro with them, you'll delight in the many fresh ways to use them. Either way, let these ideas inspire your creativity—and you, too, will experience the magic of succulents!

Each of the gardens pictured on the following pages contains ideas that can help you show off succulents with spectacular results, whether in beds, borders, or rockeries; between pavers; among tropical plants; or in desert sand. I show and explain 11 design elements, from accents and edgings to lighting your succulents at night, and I offer plenty of tips that can help you "Get the Look" in your own garden.

INSPIRATIONS

ROOF GARDEN

A SPECTACULAR VIEW of San Francisco Bay and the Golden Gate Bridge is what draws the owners up to the rooftop deck of their home in the city's Pacific Heights neighborhood. The container gardens there are like icing on the cake.

Spanning two sides of the ipe wood deck, twin planters made of powder-coated, recycled aluminum (Ore Inc.) are filled with plants that thrive in the area's often foggy, windy conditions. The owners wanted the plantings to be colorful, interesting, and water-wise. Succulents fit the bill perfectly, with big, cabbagelike rosettes of aeoniums and agaves serving as bold accents. Tall, wispy grasses that shiver nicely in the breeze provide a bit of screening without blocking the view. Now, family and friends can gather around a gas-fed firepit and enjoy the bay's panorama in a garden setting.

DESIGN IVE HAUGELAND, SHADES OF GREEN LANDSCAPE ARCHITECTURE

GET THE LOOK

The best first step to a container garden is this: Plant an *Aeonium* 'Sunburst' rosette in a low green bowl and surround it with *Sedum rupestre* 'Angelina'.

Plants with Presence

Yellow-green *Sedum rupestre* 'Angelina' fringes this planting, with variegated *Aeonium* 'Sunburst', apple green *A. undulatum*, and feathery *Asparagus densiflorus* 'Myers' behind. Feather reed grass (*Calamagrostis* x *acutiflora* 'Karl Foerster') creates the screen in back. For an immediate "grown-in effect," all plants were set close together; they're mostly from 1- and 2-gallon cans; the slow-growing *Agave attenuata* 'Variegata' is from a 5-gallon can, and the sedums, from 4-inch pots.

STYLISH SIDE YARD

CAN SUCCULENTS THRIVE in a narrow, shaded side yard that gets little, if any, care? Absolutely, as these borders alongside a home in Newport Beach, California, prove. The owner, an easygoing bachelor with little time to tend a garden, wanted low-water, low-maintenance plants to soften the narrow pathway between his home and the neighbors'.

The side yard is only about 8 feet wide; tall walls between the owner's home and the neighbors' allow little direct sunlight to reach plants. So landscape designer Molly Wood chose big, apple green aeoniums *(A. canariense)*, which she alternated with feathery, upright *Asparagus densiflorus* 'Myers' to create the narrow ribbon of low greenery edging one side of the walkway. To screen the tall wall on the other side, she selected fern pines *(Podocarpus gracilior)*, and filled in beneath them with more aeoniums and asparagus ferns. And to irrigate these plants when needed, the designer installed a drip-irrigation system that is turned off for the winter. The plants get occasional watering the rest of the year.

Wood loves the way the aeoniums grow in this low-light setting—"larger, with more open faces that are very lush green," she says. The plants' contrasting textures are striking as well, with the large, smooth leaves and sculptural shapes of the aeoniums playing off the feathery plumes of the asparagus ferns, which bob and sway in the slightest breeze.

In Southern California's warm climate, aeoniums appreciate a break from the sun and do well in lower-light locations. Keep in mind, though, that purple-leafed kinds such as *A.* 'Cyclops' won't take on the deep purple coloring in shade that they do in sunlight. Aeoniums and asparagus ferns have similar water needs: Both thrive on very little. That suits the busy bachelor just fine!

DESIGN MOLLY WOOD DESIGN

GET THE LOOK

For a similar look with a silvery color scheme, alternate grassy *Lomandra* 'Platinum Beauty' with bluish-lavender *Echeveria* 'Morning Light'.

Tunnel Vision

On both sides of the walkway, contrasting textures and shapes create interest in the all-green borders. On the left side, *Aeonium canariense* and *Asparagus densiflorus* 'Myers' fill the 6-to-12-inch-wide planting bed. On the right, where the bed is 3 to 4 feet wide, the same plants peek out from the base of the *Podocarpus* hedge. Both planting beds in this side yard are spare, and the plants in them are unfussy. That makes them great choices for busy people.

EDGINGS

Echeveria 'Imbricata' makes the perfect edging. It's easy to grow, needs little water, and stays low and compact for long periods. When planted from 2- or 4-inch containers and set 4 to 6 inches apart, echeverias will fill a space within a year.

FOR MANY YEARS, I couldn't understand why succulents were not used more frequently in landscapes. And I wondered why home gardeners chose thirsty annuals instead of beautiful, richly textured succulents to edge garden beds and borders. Recently, though, an increased need to save water in much of the West has inspired gardeners to give succulents more prominent positions in the landscape, whether as a lacy, lemony-hued fringe for a lightly shaded bed or as a bold swath of blue rosettes along a sunny garden path.

Echeverias like the ones pictured make especially beautiful edgings. Among my favorites for this use are *E. agavoides*, which has rosettes of green leaves with bronze tips; *E. colorata*, which forms stemless rosettes of thick, silvery leaves; *E.* 'Dondo', with gray-green rosettes; *E. elegans*, sometimes called Mexican snowball because of the white leaves; *E.* 'Imbricata' and *E.* 'Crinoline Ruffles', which forms rosettes of ruffly-edged leaves. All grow 3 to 6 inches tall.

Many other succulents work well as edgings. *Crassula nudicaulis platyphylla* grows about 6 inches tall, with small green leaves that pick up maroon tones as they age (the plant grows best in mild climates). *Sedum makinoi* 'Ogon', a prostrate or trailing plant, has small, rounded leaves that are plump and golden; it is excellent in shadier locations. *Sedum spathulifolium* 'Cape Blanco', a form of the Pacific Northwest stonecrop, produces small rosettes of blue-green with a powdery white coating; *S. s.* 'Purpureum', with purple-tinged leaves, takes some cold.

Patterns

This mature planting of *Echeveria* 'Imbricata' creates a cooling fringe in front of a caramel-colored *Heuchera* 'Peach Flambé', and a grasslike *Liriope* 'Silvery Sunproof', in a Palo Alto, California, garden. An 8-year-old planting, it has thrived with little care, sending out blooms every year in spring. Many echeverias will grow similarly, but with different foliage colors. *E.* 'Imbricata' freely produces offsets and spreads to form mounds 4 to 5 inches tall.

DESIGN **REBECCA SWEET**

TINY PATIO

BECAUSE HER HOUSE near the Southern California coast is set in a hillside, Leslie Mannes was short on outdoor space for get-togethers. The only possibility: a tiny, crumbling patio out back. Enter landscape designer Ryan Prange, who revamped it into a stylish, surprisingly roomy-feeling refuge. Prange repaved and planted the patio floor, tucked a seating area into the corner, and added built-in benches and a gas-fed firepit. He hid part of a broken concrete retaining wall behind a wood screen, and the rest under a curtain of creeping fig *(Ficus pumila)* planted against the wall.

"Now the patio is inviting," Prange says, "and full of nice little surprises." Among them: a small bed of sedums and silvery blue *Echeveria elegans*, mingling with blue fescue against the firepit, and ribbons of sedum between the pavers.

DESIGN RYAN PRANGE, FALLINGWATERSDESIGN.COM

GET THE LOOK

To accent a small patio, place an upright *Euphorbia trigona* in a tall 12-inch-wide ceramic pot, as shown here. Cover the soil around it with gravel mulch.

Mini Garden

Echeverias and a puff of blue fescue accent bands of sedum, visually softening the hardscape in this tiny patio.

> Some growers recommend succulents that they say can be walked on. In my experience, all succulents turn to mush when stepped on. The damaged plants may eventually grow back, but they'll look unattractive for a long time. When trampled, I can just hear those poor plants screaming "OW!"

Mixed Fillers

Echeverias accent a carpet of small sedums between these garden pavers. As both succulents grow, they'll soften the pavers' hard edges. They will also help to deter weeds.

PAVER PLANTINGS

I WAS RAISED IN THE COUNTRY near the coast of California, which probably explains my affinity for all things natural. I like soft lines, not hard edges. That's why I like to fill spaces between pavers with plants that stay small yet spread just enough to soften square edges in paths and patios.

As much as I love aeoniums and aloes, I avoid planting them between pavers; both grow too large for such confined spaces. For obvious reasons, spiky plants such as agaves should also be avoided, unless you have something evil in mind for someone like me who often wanders barefoot.

Ideally, the plants you choose to fill the space between pavers are ones that behave themselves. They don't have roots that push the pavers around, and they will not grow too aggressively. My favorites include small echeverias; small *Crassula (C. radicans, C. schmidtii)*; tiny-leafed sedums (*S. dasyphyllum, S. hispanicum*, and *S. h.* 'Purpureum'); and most of the sempervivums. Echeverias and sempervivums (hens and chicks) have rosette shapes that nest nicely between pavers. New offsets (chicks) produced by the mother plant grow out onto the pavers' surfaces, blurring the hard lines of manmade stone, but are not so aggressive that they will cover the entire paver. Smaller-leafed sedums and *Crassula* can act as groundcovers, spreading to areas where there is soil. I've used a single variety or mixed together several varieties—both with beautiful results.

At times it may be necessary to trim sedums as they grow taller than the paver surface or clamber over any rosettes nearby. Rosettes may need to be divided from time to time too as they expand their clumps.

SUCCULENTS CONTAINED

IN THE RIGHT CLIMATE, succulents will adapt to almost any challenge, including tight spaces. That's why they are the star attractions of this tiny (720-square-foot) garden in Manhattan Beach, California. As the family's only outdoor living space, the garden is packed with amenities, including designated areas for lounging and dining. Around them, the succulents and their companion plants grow in waist-high beds, like compartments in a jewel box—all are designed for close-up viewing. Tall tree aloes accent a raised bed edged with concrete beside the steps. While by the entry gate, smaller sedums spread a knobby carpet beneath grasses in the rectangular bed edged with reddish bronze Cor-ten steel. Low bowls filled with small succulents dress the tables. All are thriving— as most succulents do near the beach where the climate is mild for most of the year.

DESIGN MARK TESSIER LANDSCAPE ARCHITECTURE

View from the House

When seen from above, this garden shows off a distinct geometry, with ipe wood insets and narrow strips of low-water fescue that recall nearby boardwalks. Succulents are used in three different ways: mixed with shrubs in a raised planter beside the steps (foreground), as a groundcover beneath grasses near the entry (top), and in containers atop the tables.

GET THE LOOK

For a mod succulent garden, plant your favorite sedums by kind in four narrow beds of various lengths.

TIP

Sedums are tough to beat for their versatility. Use groundcover types in rock gardens, as bank covers, and in small areas where knobby textures are needed. Space plants 1 to 1½ inches apart. Colors include yellow (*S. makinoi* 'Ogon') and red (*S. spurium* 'VooDoo').

Living Mulch

OPPOSITE Spanish stonecrop (*Sedum hispanicum*) spreads a knobby, blue-green carpet around billowy green longleaf mat-rush (*Lomandra longifolia*) in the bed by the entry. The tiny sedum spreads slowly, but stays low (under 2 inches tall) and tidy—great for tight spaces.

Bright Bowl

ABOVE Gold-tooth aloe (*A. x nobilis*) shows off pointed, speckled leaves in a low bowl, where it makes a bold accent among silvery echeverias and smaller succulents around it. Choose young plants of this variety for low bowls. This aloe, surrounded with "pups," is starting to spread; when it gets too big for the small mixed planting, it can be easily moved elsewhere and replaced with a smaller plant.

Star-Power Plants

THIS PAGE AND OPPOSITE
A structural tree aloe
(*A. barberae*) and a beefy
coral aloe (*A. striata*) preside
over this planting beside the
entry walk. Coastal woollybush (*Adenanthos sericeus*)
provides a soft, kelplike
backdrop, while *Sedum
hispanicum* rambles around
the larger plants. Note how
the aloe is slightly tilted
outward for best viewing.

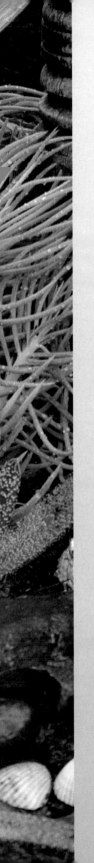

Succulent cuttings always need a few days or more to heal (form calluses on their stem ends) before you can plant them. Why not arrange them in a low bowl and enjoy them while they heal? Unlike flowers, these rosettes will look fresh for months.

Easy Accent

Succulent cuttings of various sizes and colors cluster in this giant clamshell gracing a raised bed. Tucked around it are rosettes of *Graptopetalum paraguayense* and *Sempervivum tectorum*, which resemble sea anemones, especially against the backdrop of blue-green *Aloe arborescens* 'Variegata' and *Sedum pachyphyllum*, along with kelplike *Senecio mandraliscae* and *S. cylindricus*, which appear to bend with the tide.

CONTAINERS

GROWING SUCCULENTS IN CONTAINERS has lots of advantages. As miniature gardens, they can take just minutes to put together. Succulents are adaptable, easy to work with, and so forgiving that you can move them around or replace them often, without harming roots, stems, or leaves. You can use almost any vessel that will hold soil. That piece of driftwood with a knothole you found during a beach walk? Plant the hole with *Sedum hispanicum* 'Purpureum' and watch this plant creep out and over the wood. Got a broken pot? Don't throw it away. *Crassula perfossa variegata* will look cool spilling through the break in the pot's side.

Creating succulent container gardens is fun—pure hands-in-the-dirt joy. I invited first-grade classes to the nursery to plant dish gardens. Every one of those kids got totally engaged in this therapeutic process with its nearly immediate rewards. Within an hour, the kids all went home hugging container gardens they had planted with tiny succulents that they had selected (and bonded with!).

Containers are perfect repositories for any cuttings you take while doing garden maintenance. I save empty old pots so that when I clip rosettes or branches to keep garden succulents looking their best, I can fill one of those pots with soil and stick in the cuttings. It's surprising how lovely these random plantings can turn out.

Oh, and the best part? Potted succulents are not as demanding as potted annuals. When the surf is up, you can bet that I will not be out in the garden watering! But I know that my succulents in containers will not mind; they will be just fine on their own.

INVITING ENTRY

PERCHED ON THE RIM of a coastal canyon, this property had no real landscaping in the front yard (except a wide driveway and a straight, narrow, beaten-up path to the front door) before a house remodel changed everything.

The owners wanted a wall across the front yard for security from the street, an inviting exterior facing the street, and a private courtyard behind the wall for entertaining. To match their home's new look, which they call "Napa modern," they envisioned a simple plant palette—low maintenance, low water, appealing. Succulents provided the perfect solution.

"They sent me a picture of a hotel garden they had seen and liked in La Jolla," explains landscape architect Richard Risner. "It was filled with succulents. But I didn't want to copy that garden exactly." What Risner wanted was more texture and movement, and plants that would change with the seasons. So he combined various succulents with phormiums and grasses, both outside and inside the wall. The owners were reluctant at first, he says, but now they love the succulent-grass blend.

"It's a sensory garden," says Risner. "Grasses move in the ocean breezes. And with the house windows open facing the courtyard, the owners can hear the trickle of the fountain and birds chirping in the canyon below."

DESIGN RICHARD RISNER/GROUNDED LANDSCAPE ARCHITECTURE

Street Side

Wide bands of succulents, ornamental grasses, and cactus flank the front walkway and gate. To blend with the succulents, the designer chose blue grama (*Bouteloua gracilis* 'Blond Ambition'), wild rye (*Leymus condensatus* 'Canyon Prince'), and blue oat grass (*Helictotrichon sempervirens*). The curving wall picks up the remodeled home's curves.

Bold Accent

This columnar cactus
(*Trichocereus candicans*,
also sold as *Echinopsis
candicans*), twists into
an ever-changing piece of
living sculpture as it grows.
Give it room to show off
(it will reach 4 feet tall).

Repeat Shapes

Plants with similar
shapes but varied textures
combine especially well.
This muscular Weber agave
(*A. weberi*) stands out against
the wispy wild rye and spiky
phormiums behind it.

GET THE LOOK

Try this dramatic combo in a bronze or chocolate-hued container of any size. Just pair dark rosettes, such as those of *Aeonium* 'Zwartkop', with red-tinged kalanchoe.

Interior Courtyard

OPPOSITE In the courtyard behind the front wall, a fantastic tree aloe (*A. barberae)* holds court in the raised bed. Its companions include chocolate-hued aeoniums, red-tinged paddle plant (*Kalanchoe luciae)*, and a golden barrel cactus, along with *Dudleya, Dyckia,* and echeverias.

Raised Bed

ABOVE The raised bed, custom-built of Cor-ten steel—whose patina has darkened over time to a beautiful deep rust—greets guests in the courtyard. The bed, 6½ feet long, 42 inches wide, and 18 inches high, is filled with succulents that the designer calls "Dr. Seuss looking." It makes a dynamic focal point, as does a trickling fountain near the house.

Breezy Corner

A scattering of aeoniums and aloes fills the spaces between brown phormiums and feathery green asparagus ferns in a corner of the interior courtyard, where they thrive in the light-filtered shade of a young olive tree.

CITY SLOPE

ROB LIEBERMAN AND Brian Schneider liked everything about their Victorian house in San Francisco's Castro District, except the unusable backyard, a tangled mess of greenery cloaking an uneven slope. The couple, who are both Philadelphia transplants, craved a California-style outdoor space for grilling, entertaining, and gardening.

Working with landscape designer Beth Mullins, they installed retaining walls to create three tiers that serve as outdoor rooms. The lowest level is a patio, the second is an alfresco dining room, and the third holds vegetable beds and a cutting garden. Water-wise plants fill beds throughout the garden, with succulents adding color and bold shapes to plantings in the narrow beds.

DESIGN BETH MULLINS, GROWSGREEN LANDSCAPE DESIGN

Succulent Show-offs

Pinkish purple rosettes of *Echeveria* 'Perle von Nürnberg' accent the bed of blue fescue (*Festuca glauca* 'Elijah Blue', foreground), where they stand out against green *Carex divulsa* and silvery woolly lamb's ears (*Stachys byzantina*). *Dudleya* add pops of white to both beds on the level above, where they mingle with grasses and perennials.

Bold and Breezy

ABOVE Against the soft
backdrop of wispy sedges
and silvery lamb's ears,
the *Echeveria* 'Perle von
Nürnberg' stands out—and
shows off its delicate clusters
of pink seasonal blooms.

The Finishing Touch

OPPOSITE Small echeveria
rosettes in shades of silvery
gray and soft pink mingle
with chocolate-hued aeoniums
in a low, soft gray bowl that
matches the garden's slate
gray walls. Easy arrangements
such as this go together quickly.

GET THE LOOK

No time for planting? Make an
arrangement for your outdoor
tabletop using cuttings of single
succulent rosettes. Just fill the
bowl with small gravel and poke
in the succulent stems.

CANYON VIEW

LOCATED IN THE fire-prone foothills of Santa Barbara, this front-yard garden provides a serene space for outdoor living. "We wanted to take advantage of the canyon and ocean views, and to create an enchanting approach to the house," says the designer. But the garden also needed to be water-wise, fire smart, and low-maintenance. "We used fire-resistant plants as recommended by the Santa Barbara County Fire District and incorporated plenty of defensible space— drifts of plantings instead of full-coverage plantings near the house, as recommended by Cal Fire," adds the designer.

Succulents fit the bill because of the high-moisture content of their leaves; they are clustered near the entry path and around a shapely boulder. The sea of ⅜-inch California Gold gravel mulch around these sparse plantings serves as a firebreak, while helping to show off the sculptural agaves and delicate restios. The surrounding trees have high skirts to eliminate fuel ladders.

DESIGN MARGIE GRACE/GRACE DESIGN ASSOCIATES

Set in Stone

These agaves hug a low, flat boulder against a backdrop of a shapely coast live oak *(Quercus agrifolia)*. To establish the agaves, the designer used timer-operated, hose-end driplines to water the plants "right at the wilt point"—enough to moisten the soil about 6 inches deep. "We watered every 6 weeks or so the first year, a couple of times the second year, then not at all from the third year on," she adds.

HILLSIDE LOT

"I'VE ALWAYS LOVED PLANTS, especially succulents," confesses David Perkins, owner and creator of this stylish rockery garden in the hills above Oakland, California. "And I wanted a garden that looks indigenous, with the colors and textures of the Mediterranean."

But before he could create a garden, Perkins needed to establish the yard itself. His sloping property provided no usable space to set out the natives and succulents he craved, because the hairpin turn of a winding road shaved off much of the odd, pie-shaped lot, especially in front.

Undaunted, the former firefighter dug in, terracing what little yard he could find in front, then bringing in soil and amendments to dig into the hard clay. He even drove to a quarry in Seaside, California, a couple of hours away, to buy golden granite boulders and stones, which he then trucked back to Oakland—moving some 3 to 5 tons at a time over 3 years. He placed the largest boulders first, then the smaller ones around them. "I wanted them to look like they were already there," Perkins says. He filled the spaces between them with soil, then—little by little—planted succulents, which he mixed with natives, such as salvias, and Mediterranean plants, such as thyme. To cover the ground around the plants, he chose decomposed granite mulch (¼-inch Sierra Ginger), which complements the golden granite boulders.

The garden may look finished now, but still Perkins calls it a work in progress. "I like to find out what works best, where," he says. "That's the great thing about succulents. They're easily moved. And when they're happy, they establish quickly."

They're also easy to maintain. Perkins installed a drip-irrigation system that he has never used. During droughts, he waters his plants "a bit" with the hose. "I like to travel," he says, "and I can leave town for 6 weeks, knowing that my plants will be fine."

Terraces

OPPOSITE A single *Agave* 'Blue Glow', with a lower-growing *Dudleya attenuata* on its right, accents this planting near the front door. Pink ice plant (*Oscularia deltoides*) and woolly thyme (*Thymus serpyllum*) cloak the rock walls around it. A big *Aeonium nobile* tops the wall (far left); blue-flowered *Salvia clevelandii* 'Winnifred Gilman' and red-flowered *Hesperaloe parviflora* hug the house walls above.

GET THE LOOK

Fill a depression in a single stone with a small succulent rosette. Use the planted stone to accent a border of small sedums.

TIP
To improve drainage in heavy clay soil, the owner works in Clodbuster, a blend of red lava rock, aged chicken manure, grape compost, rice hulls, and fine fir bark.

Team Players

OPPOSITE Crowded together like actors on a stage, these succulents mingle on a terrace between rock retaining walls. They include *Graptosedum* x 'Golden Glow' (foreground); a clump of orange-flowered, blue-green *Echeveria* 'Doris Taylor', whose close-set leaves are densely covered with short hairs; silvery blue *Graptoveria* 'Fred Ives'; *Aloe* 'Blue Elf', whose upright leaves have pointy tips tinged with reddish purple; and a single *Echeveria* 'Black Prince'. A patch of low, blue-green *Dymondia margaretae* spills over the rocks above.

Scene Stealer

ABOVE A bold, shapely *Agave* 'Blue Glow' accents this terraced garden planting, with *Dudleya attenuata* peeking out to its right. On the terrace above, an *Aeonium nobile* hugs a low carpet of woolly thyme *(Thymus serpyllum)*, adding a different shade of green, and hints of soft gold, to the composition.

Foliage Fountain

THIS PAGE A single *Sedum
morganianum* dangles its
long stems of plump, jelly-
bean leaves over the sides
of this tall pot, creating a
waterfall effect in the niche
of a house wall.

Mat Makers

OPPOSITE *Sempervivum*
(hens and chicks), which
spread by little offsets, make
fabulous additions to rock
gardens. They add texture as
they ramble around larger
succulents, and their offsets
dangle beautifully over
vertical stones. They need
excellent drainage to thrive.
The plants get by with just
enough water to prevent
shriveling.

Plants fill crevices by moving downward, but they seldom travel uphill. Given a choice, plant the upper part of the crevice, then allow room for the plants to grow down over time.

Stacks

Tinged with bronze, tight rosettes of *Echeveria* 'Ramillette' (cristata form) and *E. derenbergii* thrive between vertically stacked flagstones that create a low wall at Succulent Gardens Nursery in Castroville, California. Larger succulents fill the space atop the wall: They include yellow and white rosettes of *Aeonium* 'Sunburst', and variegated agaves.

DESIGN ANDREA HURD/MARIPOSA GARDENING AND DESIGN

CREVICES AND ROCK WALLS

SUCCULENTS ARE SURVIVORS in all kinds of places. But when planted in crevices between boulders or stones, they show off with style. My work with vertical gardens has been greatly inspired by how echeverias, sedums, and sempervivums grow naturally in cracks and crevices in their native habitats. There, these plants often start from windblown seeds that find their way into a crevice, then germinate and grow. Whereas seeds are tiny, installing a grown plant into a tight space takes creativity.

The easiest approach to planting succulents between stones is when the wall's stones are being stacked. For an existing wall with 1- to 2-inch crevices between stones, start with plants from 2-inch nursery pots. I remove each plant from the container, reshape its rootball to fit the space between the rocks, then use a chopstick to push the roots into the space. Finally, I fill the remaining space with soil as needed.

I have used many types of succulents in walls, but echeverias and sempervivums are my favorites for wedging between rocks. It can take a year or two for the plants to get established. Once they do, they grow and reproduce, colonizing the space given them.

Retaining walls that hold soil and plants along the top and in wall-front crevices are easiest to irrigate; water applied from above seeps downward to moisten the plants' root zones. Getting water into the crevice of a freestanding wall is more difficult. In this situation, apply water as a mist, ideally from a hose pointed toward the front, and do so slowly until water reaches the root zone. I check the soil for moisture penetration by poking in a stiff piece of wire.

VERTICAL GARDEN

WHAT HAPPENS WHEN you build an addition onto your house? Chances are, you lose square footage outdoors, as the owners of this home did on their small lot in Venice, California. Wanting to make the most of the space that remained for a serene sanctuary from the city, the couple brought in a design team to build a patio that feels like an extension of the house. Then, designer Marc Bricault came up with the idea to extend the outdoor living space by creating "gardens in the sky." He covered the walls and one rooftop of the new addition in waterproof vinyl, then attached a series of modular cells containing rooted succulents and, on the roof, grasses, yarrow, lantana, and clumps of ice plant that cover themselves with magenta blooms. Behind the railings that skirt one end of this rooftop meadow are boardwalk paths, plus a small west-facing deck for viewing evening sunsets, and tidy raised beds where the couple can grow crops. The experiment gave the couple back the greenery they'd lost—and then some.

DESIGN RICHARD GRIGSBY, GREAT OUTDOORS LANDSCAPE DESIGNS; MARC BRICAULT

Green Wall

OPPOSITE This patio may be small, but the home's new addition adds growing space: Succulents cloak its walls and roof, creating a green backdrop (and focal point) for the small patio in foreground. A vine-covered fence underlines the building's green wall, and makes a leafy backdrop for a phormium. To block views of a parking lot next door, the designers lined the fence with tall plants such as angel's trumpet and princess flower.

GET THE LOOK

This innovative planting represents thinking outside the box on a large scale. But you can create the look on a much smaller structure, such as a birdhouse (see page 161).

Workhorse Sedums

OPPOSITE Various small sedums were pre-rooted in modular cells, by ELT Easy Green (*eltlivingwalls.com*), prior to installation on the house walls and roof. The plants are watered by a drip-irrigation system.

Box Top

ABOVE Flowers and grasses enhance the planting atop the new addition. From an adjoining roof deck on the home's main portion (see photo on page 58), the owners can look west over this meadow in the sky to watch the sun set over the ocean.

GET THE LOOK
Make a stylish centerpiece for an outdoor table. Drop a sedum "tile" (see page 161) into a 12-inch square box, about 3 inches high, of ceramic or wood (drill drain holes in the bottom first).

PAINTING WITH PLANTS

THE MINUTE THAT TRAVELERS nudge their cars past the wide bend of a curving country road near Los Gatos, California, a planting so wild, so vivid and imaginative, grabs their attention such that they're forced to slow, then stop to gawk, maybe even reach for a camera. The river of ice blue *Echeveria elegans* that appears to tumble lustily along the roadside bank fronting a hillside home is pure floral fireworks. "Painting with plants" is how landscape architect Jarrod Baumann describes the process he used to design this garden. "When you love plants as much as I do, you use them like paints and paint the garden with them."

Luckily, for this project Baumann got to work with the property's equally passionate owner, a plant biologist with a weakness for succulents. She hired Baumann to convert her country-style garden into a more modern landscape. Before long, the two were bouncing ideas off one another, Baumann scribbling his on paper napkins while out in the garden. The result is a playground full of unexpected foliage and flower blends, garden art—and a little magic. "My crazy ideas come from everywhere: jewelry, plants, fashion," Baumann says. This curvy wall topped with beefy blue *Agave franzosinii*? It's a nod to the owner's native Scotland, with its many dry-stacked walls. It's Baumann's gift to the owners, and to anyone driving down the country road.

DESIGN JARROD BAUMANN/ZETERRE LANDSCAPE ARCHITECTURE

Illusion

OPPOSITE Some 3,500 plants make up this bed of *Echeveria elegans* in full bloom that appears to tumble over Mexican blue river rock. Behind, a wall inspired by the cairns (stacked stones) of Scotland is topped with beefy blue agaves (*A. franzosinii*) and brushlike *Dasylirion*, all edged with *Senecio cylindricus*.

GET THE LOOK

For a cool pool effect, set 25 plants of *Echeveria secunda*, from 4-inch pots, in a 3-by-3-foot bed. Space them 8 inches apart in staggered rows. They'll fill in within a year or two.

Shapes

THIS PAGE Spiky agaves
(*A. filifera*) carry the show
in a large, square planter
of powder-coated aluminum.
The low-growing rosettes
around them are *Echeveria*
'Lola', which send up
clusters of orange and yellow
blooms in summer.

Layers

OPPOSITE Golden barrel
cactus (*Echinocactus
grusonii*) nestle between
palm trunks, their spines
shimmering in sunlight
behind coral aloes (*A. striata*
x *saponaria)* and a fringe
of grasslike, orange-tinged
Libertia peregrinans.

TIP

For maximum impact, mix succulents of contrasting shapes and sizes but in shades of the same color, whether warm (oranges and red) or cool shades of blue.

Water-wise shrubs, perennials, and grasses make the best companions for succulents in mixed borders. The coral bells (*Heuchera*) at left and the blue fescue and smoke tree (*Cotinus*) at right are great examples. All are showy and easy to grow in a range of climates.

Tiers

ABOVE Smooth-leafed rosettes of *Echeveria elegans* edge this bed, in front of ruffly-leafed coral bells (*Heuchera*) and ornamental grasses. The tidy rows of plants, all arranged by height for easy viewing, also combine beautifully for color, with the glacial green echeverias lighting up the dark greens of the coral bells, whose rose-tinged blooms add a seasonal bonus.

Textures

OPPOSITE Smooth icy blue agaves, fringed with low clumps of brushlike blue fescue, edge the driveway in front of purple smoke tree (*Cotinus coggygria*), showing off its purple "smoke puffs." A green incense cedar drapes its branches above them.

Colors

OPPOSITE Sherbet hues of mango, lemon, and lime combine in this mixed planting, with succulents as accents. Stripes on the big, sunny face of *Aeonium* 'Sunburst' (bottom left) pick up the grassy greens behind, while *Leucadendron* 'Jester' (bottom right) echoes the coral flowers of aloes (*A. striata*) in back.

Bold Strokes

ABOVE A palm-like tree aloe (*A. arborescens*) thrives in a large square container, bringing the garden feel to a parking area near the driveway. A sea of *Senecio crassissimus* puffs out around it.

I've always been a sucker for blue-pink combos, such as these echeveria rosettes nestled in a bed of blue senecio. There's even a bit of blue in the heart of the center rosette. Nice touch!

Living Art

This colorful collage includes six species: variegated *Aeonium* 'Sunburst' (bottom left), which contrasts with the tiny green stars of *Crassula capitella thyrsiflora* 'Shark's Tooth'; a trio of rosy, ruffly-leafed *Echeveria gibbiflora* in a band of blue *Senecio serpens* (center); and yellow striped *Agave lophantha* 'Quadricolor' (top), which appears to float in the bed of greenish yellow *Sedum rupestre* 'Angelina'. Eventually, the *Crassula* will bloom, the echeverias will send out tall flower stems, and the aeoniums will grow taller—probably 2 feet above everything else.

DESIGN JOE STEAD

COLOR PAIRINGS

AS A GROWER, I always concentrated on producing succulents in a variety of shapes, colors, textures, and sizes. That's because I watched designers mix these varied types in artful ways to create spectacular beds, borders, and container plantings. I thought of my nursery as a paint store, my plants as the paints, and my inventory as the palette with which to work. The designers and home gardeners who bought my plants were the artists; they chose plants as a painter does paints—for a specific garden that became their living canvas.

A caveat: Having a vision of what you want the garden to look like in 1, 2, 3, or more years is as important as knowing what it will look like right after planting. Similar to a painter starting out with a blank canvas, you, the gardener, begin with a plot of earth and perhaps a planting scheme you have seen and admired. Even a photo can serve as your vision. Then you choose the plants to fit your vision.

When I select plants, I always consider how big they'll grow, how much they'll spread, and how long it will take for them to reach their prime. I may decide, for example, to choose three varieties for a bed 8 feet long and 4 feet wide: an *Aloe plicatilis* in a 15-gallon can; enough aeoniums *(A. canariense)* in 4-inch nursery containers to plant 12 to 15 inches apart around it; and *Aeonium* 'Cyclops' in 1-gallon cans, also to plant about 15 inches apart. Within 1 to 2 years, the aeoniums should fill in around the aloe, elevating the succulent bed to its prime time. Or I may decide on a showy mix of succulent textures and colors to arrange as a mosaic, like the one pictured here.

GARDEN GALLERY

A TINY PATIO, backed by a slope that ends in an ugly retaining wall, can be a challenging space to make beautiful. But landscape designer Brent Green did just that, by refinishing the wall behind this small patio (10 feet wide by 32 feet long) in Los Angeles to use as a striking display space for succulent pictures. Framed like art, these "paintings"—inspired by the patterns on the owners' wedding china—are filled with tiny sedums and echeverias, whose colors echo or complement the wall's new mauve hues.

Green added a low planter at the wall's base, filled it with spiky green fortnight lilies (*Dietes* 'Lemon Drops'), along with deep purple phormiums and beefy green aeoniums. Chocolate-hued 'Black Magic' elephant's ear *(Alocasia)* flanks the fountain, while golden *Acorus gramineus* fringes the front. A shrubby succulent, *Euphorbia tirucalli* 'Sticks on Fire', blazes like a fire in the mauve container.

DESIGN BRENT GREEN/GREENART LANDSCAPE DESIGN INC.

Tricks of the Trade

Succulents in these pictures are planted through pencil-thin openings in the front panels of metal "envelopes." Soil inside is a mix of perlite and vermiculite.

BEACH MODERN

UNLIKE MANY SHINGLED or clapboard cottages overlooking Monterey Bay, this beachside home in Aptos, California, is totally modern indoors and out. "The idea was to blend both spaces so they ignite each other," says architect Steve Ehrlich. "The house design is pure, simple, strong, and geometric." So the garden needed to be equally bold. Succulents are the best choices for this look.

To blend with the home's silvery grays, landscape architect Stephen Sutherland chose powdery blue agaves, icy blue senecios, and pinkish echeverias, which he arranged in blocks to complement the home's strong lines. Ornamental grasses, placed in equally wide ribbons, add a softening effect. "I wanted to create a landscape that both enhances the architectural style of the house and creates seamless living from indoors to out," he says.

The owners, Leland and Marian Zeidler, are thrilled with the results. They both are passionate collectors of modern art, which they now display indoors and in their garden. "I like big sweeps of a few different plants for a simple, uncluttered look," says Leland. What do they like most? "It's low maintenance," says Marian. "And it really works."

DESIGN STEPHEN SUTHERLAND/SSA LANDSCAPE ARCHITECTURE (GARDEN); STEVE EHRLICH/ STEVE EHRLICH ARCHITECTS (HOME)

Artistic Touches

Angles and shapes play out in both the house and the garden, where the succulents are arranged in distinct bands behind a sea of blue fescue. The metal sculpture is by local artist Kenneth Hepburn. The owners had it painted red to protect it from moisture.

Mod Border

Along the side of the house, bands of blue fescue (*Festuca glauca* 'Elijah Blue') and coppery-hued *Carex testacea* fringe a low border of *Agave attenuata* 'Nova'. Each agave is a living sculpture, which delights the owners, who view the plants through windows as a backdrop for their indoor art. To create this planting, Stephen Sutherland used the following: blue fescue (from 1-gallon cans), spaced 14 inches apart; *Carex testacea* (1 gallon), 18 inches apart; and agaves (5 gallon), 24 inches apart.

Living Sculpture

ABOVE A fan aloe (*A. plicatilis*), fringed with bluish *Senecio serpens*, shows off its uniquely sculptural shape beside the front door. The owners' fondness for this living sculpture is only going to grow as the plant matures over time. The container planting reflects in the shimmery glass to the left, while the rich wood doorway provides a perfect contrast to set off its shape. A carpet of blue fescue (foreground) adds softness and blends with the colors of the aloe and glass.

Pink Fringe

OPPOSITE The property's low front wall is softened by this 50-foot-long planting of pinkish lavender *Echeveria* 'Afterglow' rosettes, backed by taller stems of *Senecio crassissimus*. The echeverias (from 1-gallon cans) were set about 4 inches apart; they're neatly lined up "like little soldiers," Leland says, and they've produced offsets to create the densely packed look. Plants of *Senecio crassissimus* (from 1-gallon cans) were set 6 inches apart.

GET THE LOOK

To accent a small patio, plant a 6-inch *Senecio crassissimus* in the center of a circular, 3-foot-diameter bed. Set six plants of 6-inch *Echeveria* 'Afterglow' around it.

> I was once so inspired by a book called *Maya Color* that I painted several walls at my nursery in bold colors. Vivid colors really do bring out qualities of the plants that you display in front of them.

Fountain of Foliage

Agave desmettiana 'Variegata' shows off its fountain-like form against a hot red wall. Blue *Senecio mandraliscae* carpets the ground beneath it; as it grows, the stems spill over the planter's edge, creating a waterfall effect above the pool (the senecio needs periodic pruning to stay above the waterline). The planter, about 3½ feet wide and 24 feet long, has a built-in French drain and a weep hole at the right side to drain water away. A drip-watering system, installed before planting, keeps the plants irrigated.

ACCENTS

DRIVING HOME ONE DAY from California's Central Valley, I spotted an ancient barn with a big old prickly pear cactus growing next to it. The two posed so artfully together that they stopped me in my tracks. I had to turn around and go back to admire them close up.

Many succulents are so sculptural that they beg a place in the spotlight. A tall *Aloe barberae*, with a trunk like a palm tree and long, graceful leaves atop curving stems, is an example. Plant it in front of a light-colored stucco wall, and it becomes the eye-catching star of a garden, with all the presence of a diva on stage. (Amp up the drama by lighting it at night to throw shadows on the wall behind; see page 124.) All the tree aloes, including *A. ferox* and *A. speciosa*, as well as columnar cactus, euphorbias, and yuccas, can create spectacular effects when displayed in this manner.

Strong statements in the landscape can be made by smaller plants as well. Spiral aloe *(A. polyphylla)* is one of the most striking plants in the succulent world. The leaves' spiral arrangement needs to be viewed from directly above, or tilted toward the viewer.

Other succulents, such as *Dasylirion longissimum*, are stunning when viewed at eye level, or higher. I once planted two agaves *(A. weberi)* in wide, low containers, which I displayed atop 8-foot-tall pillars on both sides of a driveway. The agaves made beautiful silhouettes against the blue sky. Colored walls are also great backdrops for sculptural succulents.

PATTERNS

"THERE'S NO WAY to duplicate a natural setting," says landscape architect Keith Willig of this property, edging a creek. But Willig didn't want to mimic the creek area, either. Nor did the property's owners, who love the minimalist aesthetic of their home. Instead, Willig played up the leafy wildscape edging the creek through contrast. He used structural plants to extend the home's architectural geometry into the yard and then loosened up the design toward the garden's perimeter near the creek.

Succulents are grouped by kind in tidy circular and rectangular beds, all surrounded with gravel mulches in various hues, from beige to soft gray. Now the owners' minimalist crush extends to the yard, which changes with the seasons. The succulent blooms come and go; the grasses get big seed plumes. And the garden feels like a work of art.

DESIGN KEITH WILLIG/KEITH WILLIG LANDSCAPE ARCHITECTURE AND CONSTRUCTION

Squares

Wild around the edges (those chairs face the creek), this garden is a streamlined sanctuary. Beds in bold, geometric shapes show off succulents that are massed, by variety, to enhance the garden's minimalist look. A wide path filled with taffy gravel winds around the beds. It's dotted with concrete pavers that look like cross sections of eucalyptus logs (from San Francisco's Flora Grubb Gardens). Tightly packed rosettes of *Echeveria* 'Afterglow' grow in the foreground.

Lines

ABOVE Succulents and
cactus—including *Aloe ferox*,
variegated *Agave americana*
'Mediopicta Alba', and spiny
barrel cactus *(Ferocactus)*—
stand out in long, narrow beds
against the home's cedar
siding. Silvery pink echeverias
(*E.* 'Afterglow') and a blue-
green *Carex divulsa* grow in
the foreground. All plants
in the garden are water-wise
and seldom need irrigation.

Circles

OPPOSITE Framed with
pale gray gravel mulch,
the agaves (*A.* 'Blue Glow')
in this circular bed are
widely spaced to allow for
growth and to show off
their structural shapes.
Lacy-leafed birch trees,
underplanted with asparagus
ferns (*A. densiflorus* 'Myers'),
create a delicate backdrop.

GET THE LOOK

To duplicate this circle of
agaves, set 8-inch plants of
A. 'Blue Glow' 16 to 20 inches
apart within a circular bed.
These solitary plants do
not produce offsets.

Graphics

OPPOSITE Neat rosettes of *Echeveria* 'Afterglow' are arranged shoulder-to-shoulder in a raised bed, edged with blue river rock and taffy-colored gravel. Small enough to view up close, the bed resembles a living picture, or knobby carpet, spread out on the ground.

Glow

ABOVE Edged with thin red bands and inner gold bands, the leaves of *Agave* 'Blue Glow' light up when backlit by the sun. The leaves are spineless, but have very sharp tips, a good reason to provide plenty of space around them. These plants seldom produce offsets, making them ideal for creating sculptural effects.

GET THE LOOK

In a garden bed, set out plants of *Echeveria* 'Afterglow' from 4-inch containers; space them so their centers measure 6 to 12 inches apart. They'll fill in within a year or two.

MINIMALIST "DOTS"

BRIAN KISSINGER HATES clutter. Blame it on growing up in a house full of knickknacks—his parents were antique dealers. That's one reason the landscape designer and horticulturist was attracted to the 1960s modern house he shares with partner Todd McCandless. The home's clean lines inspired the garden renovations. Kissinger's mantra: Provide enough detail to make the garden feel like a relaxing retreat, but not one iota more.

His bed of golden barrel cactus *(Echinocactus grusonii)* is as bold and graphic as it is restful to look at. The tidy arrangement gives the plants a fresh, contemporary spin. Solid though the cactus appear, they bring magic to the garden when backlit by the sun, or when they cast shadows across the gravel mulch, which soften, lengthen, and move on with the day.

Well-spaced plants, arranged by kind, are more calming than a chaotic jumble of different types. You can appreciate each one's form more easily. Less clutter, less stress—isn't that what we all crave?

DESIGN BRIAN KISSINGER

GET THE LOOK

For a bold effect in a smaller space, plant three barrel cactus, about 20 inches apart, in front of a shapely boulder backed by rosemary. Mulch the soil with gold gravel.

Spacing

Give the stars of each bed, such as these barrel cactus, enough room to show off (say, 4 or 5 feet), and then restrict the supporting cast to a limited selection of plants that complement them. Here, a few sculptural boulders edge the bed. The plantings behind them are both soft and sculptural, with fanlike foliage repeating throughout. They include agaves, purplish opuntias, bristly yuccas, and a soft carpet of rosemary.

Groundcover succulents look especially pretty when you let various kinds, in contrasting colors, ramble together. At times, it will be necessary to prune the more aggressive varieties.

GROUND-COVERS

FOR MANY YEARS, succulent groundcovers were confined to the different varieties of ice plant, members of the *Mesembryanthemum* family. The state of California filled freeway medians with *Carpobrotus edulis*, often referred to as "freeway ice plant," whose brilliant, purplish pink blooms nearly glowed along highways in spring. Remnants of these plantings still grow throughout the state.

Now, the palette of groundcover types has expanded to include many other succulents in a wide range of textures and colors, from the tiny-leafed, very low-growing European sedums to the more aggressive, larger-leafed *Crassula*, *Graptopetalum*, and senecios. Among my favorites for bold effects: *Sedum nussbaumerianum* and *S.* × *rubrotinctum* 'Aurora', *Senecio mandraliscae*, *Graptopetalum paraguayense*, *Crassula thyrsiflora* 'Campfire', and *Oscularia deltoides*. Use these plants as inexpensive fillers in beds and borders; most will create a carpet effect within a year if planted 6 to 15 inches apart, depending on the variety. In most cases, plants from 4-inch nursery pots will do the trick, but 1-gallon containers will work for the wider spacing. Cell-packs need more frequent waterings to establish their shallow roots.

I like mixing different groundcovers, giving each patch 6 to 30 square feet (more if you have the space), then watching them grow together to form a colorful mosaic. Some varieties stay quite low; others form mounds 6 to 15 inches tall. Larger specimens, such as taller agaves and aloes, look especially interesting when interspersed among lower types.

Living Mosaic

A patch of vibrant, orange-tinged *Crassula thyrsiflora* 'Campfire', accented with a taller *Euphorbia tirucalli* 'Sticks on Fire', contrasts with icy blue, ground-hugging *Senecio mandraliscae*, which wanders through the garden and along the pathway. The *Senecio* and *Crassula* need pruning each spring to stay clear of paths nearby.

DESIGN AMELIA B. LIMA

BEAUTIES AT THE BEACH

THIS SMALL GARDEN takes its design cues from the nearby beach. Throughout the lot, various outdoor rooms are filled with succulents and other unthirsty plantings, all inspired by coastal flora. Drought tolerant and requiring little maintenance, the plants always look tidy.

In the front yard, inviting steps lead to the front door with stops along the way: at the firepit and at a cozy gathering spot on the porch. The backyard, which also evokes a coastal feeling, has areas for lounging, soaking in the hot tub, and dining. Throughout the front and backyard gardens, succulents are stars in little vignettes that have big impact. All plants are on a timer-operated drip-irrigation system, with tubing laid atop the soil and covered with mulch.

DESIGN RYAN PRANGE, FALLINGWATERSDESIGN.COM

Beach-scape

A pair of agaves adds a sculptural element among grasses near the entry walk (foreground). A third agave accents the bed beside the front porch steps. Agaves are tough to beat for pure drama among grasses and perennials such as yellow yarrow (*Achillea*), which also blooms near the firepit.

GET THE LOOK

As this *Crassula* ages, prune its lowest branches to reveal the stout trunk. A blue river rock mulch is the perfect finishing touch.

Reef Shapes

ABOVE Golden jade tree (*Crassula ovata* 'Hummel's Sunset') shows off its spreading canopy and thick, coral-reef-like trunk. This plant grows slowly to 2 to 3 feet tall; golden yellow foliage is sometimes tinged with red, mostly during cooler months. (Expect it to be mostly green after repotting or overfeeding the plant.) In hot desert areas, place it in a cool northern exposure.

Estuary Greens

OPPOSITE Small green sedums, along with *Senecio cylindricus* and echeveria rosettes, shimmer at the base of the front-yard firepit. Plants such as these are nearly indispensable for softening hard edges around paving and natural stones. The gas-fed firepit, made of buff-colored Mexican beach cobbles and boulders set in mortar, is embellished with shells. It is filled with sand that's then topped with pieces of shell. This little vignette "brings the beach to the house and gives the garden a sense of place," says the designer.

Boardwalk View

OPPOSITE Tucked between the back yard's hot tub and redwood deck, a sculptural agave and clusters of echeverias mingle with colorful yarrows *(Achillea)*. This bed, along with the change in level here, helps to visually separate the lounge area from the lower dining area, a trick that makes small gardens appear larger. A rock wall fringed with Berkeley sedge divides the upper deck from the dining area in the foreground. At night, strings of bistro lights emit a soft glow, like starlight, above the hot tub.

Dune Blooms

ABOVE The tidy cluster of *Echeveria* rosettes in the "center stage" bed nestles against a sand-colored boulder with yellow yarrow and Berkeley sedge in a small planting bed—made for viewing from the hot tub and the nearby deck.

GET THE LOOK

Dudleya is truly spectacular; display it singly in a porous container that helps roots breathe. When planting, tilt the rosette to one side for best viewing.

Succulent Seascape

TOP LEFT Plants in various shapes and sizes create striking contrasts in this vignette beside a garden path. Dragon tree *(Dracaena draco)* fans out its bristly, silver-gray leaves above a single *Agave attenuata*, while fine-textured, dark green *Carex divulsa* weaves a soft carpet between them. Yarrow *(Achillea millifolium)* adds pops of yellow.

Coastal Native

TOP RIGHT *Dudleya brittonii* peeks over the rim of a terra-cotta pot on the deck. This silvery beauty has wide-leafed rosettes on stems that gradually lengthen to 1- to 2-foot trunks. It grows best near the coast, needs bright light, and thrives in rock gardens and containers, as shown here.

Ocean Blues

BOTTOM LEFT Nestled between a boulder and a turn in the garden path, this grouping of succulents in luscious, eye-candy colors begs a closer look. The plants include *Echeverias*— *E.* 'Perle von Nürnberg', *E.* 'Blue Wren', and other hybrids. A chalky white, fine-leafed finger aloe *(Cotyledon orbiculata oblonga)* grows in the center; the silvery green groundcover at bottom right is *Dymondia margaretae*.

Tidepool Planting

A cluster of chocolate-hued aeonium rosettes accents this bed near the backyard dining area. Blue-green prostrate juniper (*Juniperus procumbens* 'Nana') and golden *Acorus gramineus* 'Ogon' grow around it, brightening the planting with contrasting color and texture. Mexican beach pebbles fill the spaces between pavers.

Aeoniums and aloes make great accents among fine-textured grasses. They look a little ghostlike when settled among grasses that sway in the breeze.

Beachside Beauties

Clusters of *Aeonium canariense* ramble around gnarly-trunked Monterey cypress trees and among grasses (California field sedge and *Leymus* 'Canyon Prince') in this beachfront meadow in Carmel, California. A seascape in the background is about as good as it gets for me. Another way to describe this: Succulents, grass, and surf—I'm in my element!

DESIGN **BERNARD TRAINOR**

MEADOWS

TRY GOOGLING "ALOES IN HABITAT," and you will learn that these succulents commonly grow in native grasslands in South Africa. Bold succulents and delicate ornamental grasses look great together. The grasses shimmer in sunlight and shiver in breezes, adding beauty and motion around the more structured plants.

I'm especially fond of aloes such as Cape aloe *(A. ferox)* and *A. striatula* for this use, because they grow tall enough to show above the grasses. When these aloes flower, their candelabras of orange and yellow flowers rise over the softer grass tips, with spectacular effects. The best grasses for pairing with these succulents are low, clumping, drought-tolerant kinds such as blue grama *(Bouteloua gracilis* 'Blond Ambition') and dropseed *(Sporobolus).*

To create these mixed meadows, I buy aloes that already have a head start on growth, so they will show above the grasses after just a year. I set them at least 2 to 3 feet apart. Then I plant the grasses in widely spaced clusters around them.

Newly planted grasses need a fair amount of water, so I irrigate them deeply for the first few months to establish their roots. Then I slowly wean them off the water. (Aeoniums and aloes both tolerate watering during that time frame.) Spring and fall are good times to plant; avoid the hot summer months.

HIGH DESERT RANCH

TROY WILLIAMS AND Gino Dreese, who are both landscape professionals in the Palm Springs, California, area, love rocks and cactus, which are plentiful in the high desert. They make good use of these elements around their getaway home in the Mojave Desert. Gardening conditions can be brutal here —"exposed" as Williams calls them: hot in the summer, cold in the winter, with fierce afternoon winds March through May. The low deserts of Palm Springs, where they do most of their work, "are easy," says Williams. "The high desert is difficult."

Still, golden barrel cactus *(Echinocactus grusonii)* thrives here; it always provides bright color. Williams and Dreese planted it in blocks or mixed it with other succulents, including agaves—*A. parryi* does extremely well here. Opuntias and chollas add color and sculptural forms, as do saguaros *(Carnegiea gigantea)*. Ocotillos *(Fouquieria splendens)* root slowly, but do well once established, and they provide beautiful flowers each spring.

"Our house sits on a natural rock outcrop, and there is very little soil," explains Williams. "So we use livestock troughs for many plantings. We place a trough where we want it, fill it with native decomposed granite and sand, then build up native rocks around it to hide and insulate it. In troughs, the water we give the plants lasts longer." Williams and Dreese can almost watch the plants grow if they water a couple of times a week during the summer and fertilize the plants a few times a year.

GET THE LOOK

Plant three golden barrels around an attractive rock, with a columnar cactus in back, for a quick and easy small-area cactus garden.

Bowled Over

Golden barrel cactus fill rock-edged beds that flank the rustic Mojave Desert ranch house. A columnar saguaro accents the foreground bed, while ocotillos fan out their upright, twiggy branches behind. To keep the barrel cactus clean of dust caused by winds, Williams and Dreese irrigate the plants with a hose and wash them off at the same time.

Splashes of Pink

OPPOSITE Clusters of penstemons *(P. thurberi)*, native to the Joshua Tree National Park area, unfurl their vivid pink blooms in April or May among the golden barrel cactus. In years of above-normal rainfall, a wider variety of wildflowers sprouts here as well, showing off their delicate beauty against the bolder golden barrels, saguaros, and bayonet leaves of the young Joshua tree *(Yucca brevifolia)*.

Garden View

ABOVE The view toward the garden through the home's open front door is worth framing: It visually connects the interior to the plantings outdoors and the wildland beyond. Williams and Dreese enhanced the view by sticking empty wine bottles through wall panels on either side of the door. The bottles are about a foot long and provide insulation as well as interesting lighting as the sun shines through them.

GET THE LOOK
Compose your garden to fit a view. Curve the beds' edges, then group smallest succulents in foreground, tallest "eye-catchers" in back.

To accent a dry border, try this: Plant a smoldering red *Aloe cameronii* at the base of a rugged, earth-toned boulder. The stone can act as a frame for the succulent, elevating it to a living work of art. To complete the picture, cover the ground around it with a mulch of neutral-toned decomposed granite.

Urban Modern

Bronze-tinged *Echeveria agavoides* rosettes form a tidy, rounded clump in front of a much larger rusted mechanical pulley, its bottom partially submerged in soil topped with decomposed granite mulch. Completing this play on circles, in a display garden at the San Francisco International Airport that the designer calls Modern Urban Industrial, are rusted pipe flanges and strainer caps, salvaged from SFO's metal dump.

DESIGN MEL HARRINGTON

FOILS

IN GARDENS, a foil can be a big boulder or a found object that, when placed behind or beside a succulent, highlights the plant in some way, turning it into a horticultural version of the exclamation point. Succulents pair incredibly well with a vast array of objects because they are adaptable and diverse in their shapes and colors, and because they grow into, over, and around objects so naturally.

I'm a big fan of planting succulents, especially shapely agaves, in front of boulders where their bold forms and smooth green leaves can stand out. I also like to place boulders where they'll retain soil above ground level, then plant aeoniums or *Graptopetalum* on top and let them cascade down the face of the stone.

I've used many repurposed items as foils: a broken pot tilted on its side and spilling echeverias, a child's dump truck loaded with sedums and sempervivums, plow discs, too shallow for any other type of plant to survive but overflowing with succulents. The discs and succulents looked made for each other, and the combination showed off how adaptable the succulents are.

I've often thought strawberry jars are misnamed, because they make perfect foils for succulents. Small sedums and other shapely kinds thrive in those small side pockets and show off their shapes as they might in the crevice of a cliff face. Aeoniums and echeverias grow large enough to fill the opening on top. I say "succulent jars" is a more appropriate name.

WINE COUNTRY ROCKERY

A NATURAL ROCK OUTCROP, adjacent to a venerable oak tree, inspired the original owners of this property, near Napa, California, to plant succulents among the stacked, lichen-encrusted boulders. The plants grew and thrived, weaving a knobby tracery of green between the boulders. The effect was so striking that the landscape architects, hired by the property's current owners, decided to keep the rockery intact and design a garden around it that complements the planting. Now, the rockery—planted with sedums and *Graptopetalum paraguayense*—serves as a welcoming portal to the pool area, along with the beautifully sculptural oak across the path. The sedums that fringe the rockery can take the summer heat and winter cold of the Napa hills and produce bright yellow flowers in the late spring. The silvery foliage of *Graptopetalum* blends nicely with the lichens growing on the rocks.

DESIGN IVE HAUGELAND/SHADES OF GREEN LANDSCAPE ARCHITECTURE

Napa Natural

Pavers planted with grass practically point to the rocky outcrop and help it to blend with the natural setting. The succulent-covered rockery looks as though planted by nature.

ISLAND-STYLE SUCCULENTS

DAVIS DALBOK IS ENAMORED of gardens so much that he owns two—one in Northern California's Marin County and the other in Pahoa, near the southern tip of Hawaii's Big Island. "Call it gardening with one foot in the tropics and one foot in California," says the award-winning landscape designer and owner of Living Green Design in San Francisco. But it's in his Hawaii garden, filled with palms, lychee trees, and assorted plants he calls Jurassic-looking, that he finds a special joy.

Succulents are everywhere on this island property he named Hale Mohalu, whether tucked up against cycads or black lava rock. "They blend seamlessly with more tropical planting schemes," says Dalbok. And they thrive, despite the area's 175 inches of annual rainfall.

"There is a misconception that succulents don't like water," Dalbok explains. "They love water. They are made up mostly of water. But because of the very porous volcanic soils in Hawaii, the rainfall percolates down through it very quickly, so the succulents' roots never experience sitting water. Well-drained soil is key." Because it's so warm in the Puna, near the southern tip of the Big Island where Pahoa is located, he says, succulents there never experience the conditions that can spell the demise of the same plants in Northern California: wet conditions combined with low temperatures.

Dalbok describes his Hawaii garden as an "evolutionary work in progress." So he works and reworks it, taking pleasure in the process. "I'm never more content than when I spend the full day gardening here. Starting with a sunrise ocean swim, ending with a tropical cocktail on the stone veranda while looking out over all that I have had a hand in creating that day—that's pure happiness."

DESIGN DAVIS DALBOK/LIVING GREEN DESIGN

Lava Bed

Tucked beside a sprawling, black volcanic rock, a cluster of blue-green agaves (*A. attenuata*) add cool contrast to small bromeliads (*Neoregelia*), whose red leaves mimic hot lava. Both just glow after big periods of rainfall, says Dalbok. Giant fishtail palm (*Caryota obtusa*) rises behind, while a smaller palm (*Pinanga coronata*) fringes the foreground.

Repetition is key to a really great border. Before planting, set the biggest, most dramatic succulents —whether aloes or furcraeas—atop the soil, arranging them in clusters of three, or singly, along the length of the border. Move them around until you like the look, then plant. Fill in around them with smaller plants.

Foliage Fans

OPPOSITE This majestic succulent, *Furcraea selloa marginata*, shows off its gorgeous, sword-shaped leaves between a veil of wispy grasses, front, and a tall cycad *(Dioon spinulosum)*, rear. In this garden, *Furcraea* are stars of a mostly green border; they are not for small gardens, though: This variety can eventually form a 5-foot-tall trunk and spread 6 feet wide. The leaves are edged with thin strips of creamy yellow and have hooked teeth. But as accents in big foliage borders, they're tough to beat.

Great Greens

ABOVE This border is anything but boring. Plants have varied shapes, sizes, and textures. The big, round *Furcraea selloa marginata* contrast nicely with the gnarly branches and flat-topped canopy of the tall poinciana tree *(Delonix regia)* in back. "I first became aware of *Furcraea* during a visit to Roberto Burle Marx's home, Sítio Santo Antônio da Bica, north of Rio de Janeiro," says Dalbok. "I emulate his style, featuring swirly drifts of one species with drifts of companion plants at different heights wiggled in. Burle Marx is my hero!"

GET THE LOOK

For special effects, select plants whose forms echo one another, like these "foliage fans," for instance, then layer them in borders—lowest in front to tallest in back.

Jungle Companions

ABOVE From a distance, this big, purplish bromeliad (*Alcantarea imperialis* 'Merlot') might be mistaken for a succulent. It's just as bold, and its leaves are almost as stiff as some agaves. That's why it makes a perfect companion for agaves in Dalbok's garden. Here, it spreads its leaves, palm-like, above smaller bromeliads (*Neoregelia carolinae* 'Variegata'). A green-leafed cycad forms the backdrop.

Palm Shapes

OPPOSITE Most of the plants in this scene-stealing center bed—tucked against a backdrop of various palms—have something in common: shape. Their leaves appear to burst from their center stems like fireworks in the night sky. A silvery blue *Agave attenuata* accents this bed of bromeliads, which includes *Alcantarea imperialis* 'Merlot' (native to eastern Brazil), with a yellow-orange croton behind it. Lower bromeliads, whose leaves are brushed with pink, coral, or yellow, edge the bed.

ILLUSION

Too deep for comfort? Plant a tidepool garden. Fill a low bowl with cactus mix and several small agave hybrids that mimic starfish. Finish with a rock or two, mulch with aquarium pebbles, then display on an outdoor table.

Undersea Garden

Rugged boulders and mulch of sand and gravel set the scene for "marine life" plants in this Undersea Succulent Garden, at the San Diego Botanic Garden. Green *Crassula* 'Imperialis' and blue *Senecio serpens* grow in the foreground, where they appear to move with the tide. Dark green *Euphorbia caput-medusae* cloak the rocks like barnacles (middle left), and starfish-shaped *Aloe ciliaris* appear to swim over the boulder to the right. Hugging the big boulder behind are clusters of brown aeoniums (*A.* 'Jack Catlin'), which mimic sea anemones; orange *Euphorbia tirucalli* 'Sticks on Fire', which resemble coral; and a branching jade plant (middle right).

DESIGN **JEFF MOORE**

AS A LIFELONG SCUBA DIVER and snorkeler, I have had the opportunity to visit some pretty exotic areas of the world. On one trip, to the Solomon Islands, I snorkeled with three friends off uninhabited islands. While drifting through the pristine waters among giant sea fans, colorful coral beds, and all of the wonderful sea life the tropics has to offer, I was constantly reminded of the shapes and colors of the succulents back at my nursery.

So many succulents mimic undersea plants—with their rich colors and diverse, sometimes bizarre shapes—that gardeners use them to create the illusion of coral reefs in a blue lagoon. Without a doubt, designer Jeff Moore has made the most notable undersea gardens, a concept he is credited with developing. Moore, owner of Solana Succulents Nursery, has planted many such gardens, including the Undersea Succulent Garden at the San Diego Botanic Garden, which uses water-smart succulents to simulate a tropical coral reef overflowing with marine life.

Whether you live on the shore or just dream of the sea and want to re-create the look, here are some plants to consider: *Echeveria* 'Crinoline Ruffles', whose ruffle-edged rosettes look like anemones; crested *Myrtillocactus*, which resemble sea fans; *Senecio mandraliscae* and *Kalanchoe luciae*, which as they grow appear to bend and float with the currents, like kelp; and *Euphorbia caput-medusae* and *E. tirucalli* 'Sticks on Fire' for their coral-like forms. Red sunset aloe *(A. dorotheae)* or *Dyckia* 'Silver Superstar', a silvery succulent with flattened rosettes of narrow, pointed leaves, could pass for sea stars. Together, these plants can transport you to a world beneath the sea—the kind a diver might view through a mask.

DESERT "NATURAL"

IN CALIFORNIA'S COACHELLA VALLEY, the natural vegetation is both spare and lush, with widely spaced cactus and yuccas rising from the low desert's windblown sands and dunes, palm oases tucked into moist, shaded canyons, and rounded boulders casting shadows across dry, gravelly riverbeds in the harsh sun. That's exactly the "sense of place" look that Marc Walters wanted in his Palm Springs garden. "I did not want grass and flowers," he says. "There is no grass in the wild around here. I wanted this garden to look like nature planted it."

When Walters purchased the house, a low (2-foot) retaining wall and a row of wispy olive trees divided the front yard from the street. "I like a garden that's visible from the street," he says. "It looks friendlier, more inviting." Working with Marcello Villano, a former Hollywood set designer turned landscape designer, he had the "barrier" wall and the olive trees removed to open up the yard. The land was gently contoured—just enough to make it look real, says Walters—then boulders were brought in, and a drip-irrigation system installed.

The plants are widely spaced among the softly rounded boulders, so that their sculptural shapes can be appreciated. Some of the trees and shrubs are illuminated at night—"just the right amount of light without overdoing it, like Las Vegas," says Walters. During the day, the play of sunlight through the bristly desert spoon and the golden barrel cactus spines takes over, creating a natural light show.

Now, the garden looks as though it was lifted intact from the wild, just as Walters envisioned. "It gives me a sense of peace when I drive up to the house," he says.

DESIGN MARCELLO VILLANO/MARCELLO VILLANO GARDEN DESIGN

GET THE LOOK

To show off desert plants best, avoid crowding them. And cover the ground around them with fine beige gravel.

Light Show

OPPOSITE A trio of bristly *Yucca decipiens* plants adds glow and texture behind a majestic California fan palm (*Washingtonia filifera*) and a cluster of golden barrel cactus (*Echinocactus grusonii*). In front of the palm, *Aloe ferox* and a bluish, brushlike *Yucca rostrata* cozy up to the boulders, while desert spoon (*Dasylirion wheeleri*) fans out its stiff, bluish gray leaves just left of the palm. A Mexican fence post cactus (*Pachycereus marginatus*) brushes house eaves in back. As the sun moves over the garden throughout the day, the plants' varied textures and shapes create a spectacular natural light show.

Wide Spacing

Spacing them wide apart allows the blue agaves, barrel cactus, and opuntia (nearest the palms) to show off. The twiggy ocotillo (*Fouquieria splendens*) blooms in spring.

Seasonal Accent

This aloe sends up vibrant red blooms in winter. Where space is tight, try a compact type such as *A.* 'Blue Elf' or coral aloe (*A. striata*).

Desert View

OPPOSITE This planting looks as inviting as the starting point of a desert canyon trail; the low blue agaves and golden barrel cactus appear to lead toward the taller plants behind, including the bulbous-trunked bottle palm (*Beaucarnea recurvata*), center, with a small *Euphorbia resinifera* (which the locals call "witches fingers"), near its base, and the fan palms (*Washingtonia filifera* and *W. robusta*) in back. The smooth white boulders and the gray gravel mulch help all the plants to stand out.

Mirror Image

ABOVE A square, low-slung pool near the home's entry reflects in its still waters the stately silhouettes of nearby palms and columnar cactus. It also underscores the view of agaves and golden barrel cactus scattered among boulders behind, and enhances the play of light through the garden at various times of day.

The best lighting for sculptural succulents usually requires the services of an expert to install. Ask about the choices for the effect you want. One option: low-voltage lights placed at the plants' base.

NIGHT LIGHTING

I ONCE DESIGNED A SUCCULENT GARDEN on a Los Altos hilltop, in the San Francisco Bay Area, where I arranged sculptural plants such as agaves, aloes, barrel cactus, columnar cactus, and yuccas among large boulders and tall stones. I had little time to spend admiring the garden the moment we finished planting it, though, because I had to return to work in the nursery. It wasn't until the owners invited me back a few months later, for an evening reception to celebrate and enjoy their garden, that I truly discovered its magic.

As the sky darkened, garden lights came on. The cactus and succulents, lit from below, created pure drama as their shadowy forms washed, ghostlike, against stone, walls, and paving. Even the golden barrel cactus came alive as their spines cast shadows across their green bodies. I knew that these plants would be beautiful where they were placed, but I had no idea what effect the lighting would have on them. It was an evening sculpture exhibit that I will never forget.

Now, my go-to plants for nighttime drama include the following: agaves *(A. filifera* and *A. franzosinii)*; aloes such as *A. plicatilis* and tree aloes *(A. barberae, A. ferox,* and *A. marlothii)*; *Dasylirion wheeleri* and *D. longissimum*; and *Yucca rostrata.*

Shadow Play

Lights beneath these tree aloes wash over the plants' graceful trunks and cast shadowy silhouettes on the walls edging this poolside patio in Los Angeles. *Phormium* 'Jack Spratt' grows between them. Filling the bed behind them are larger phormiums, along with kangaroo paw, grasses such as variegated *Miscanthus sinensis condensatus,* and *Yushania maling,* a delicate clumping bamboo.

DESIGN R. MICHAEL SCHNEIDER

Succulents are so adaptable that you can use them in many ways: as flowerlike cuttings for indoor arrangements or wedding bouquets, as tiny rooted plants for making living pictures, as embellishments for birdhouses. On the following pages, you'll find fresh ideas and inspiration for making bouquets, seasonal wreaths, tabletop centerpieces, and more, to get your creative juices flowing. Then check out my DIY projects, such as small succulent bouquets for display in natural rock vases, and other projects created by my favorite designers, including party favors and gift wraps. All are so easy you can make them in minutes.

EASY PROJECTS

Hanging cones
(see page 180
for instructions)

ARRANGEMENTS

BECAUSE SUCCULENTS STORE THEIR OWN water, they can be cut and used in arrangements, without water, yet remain fresh for long periods of time. Eventually the cuttings will grow roots and can be planted. Succulent flowers will hold up in bouquets for a while as well, but they will not root and grow like the cuttings. And just as my wife knows when her roses will begin to bloom, I have learned what time of year succulent flowers and cuttings will be at their best for use in bouquets.

Some of my favorite succulent flowers grow from *Echeveria gibbiflora* hybrids, which flower primarily summer into fall. *Crassula falcata* can be counted on to produce scarlet flowers in fall, whereas aloes bloom in winter, when many other plants are dormant. Aloe flowers range from orange and yellow to red, depending on the variety.

Cuttings of most succulents can be used in bouquets, but I choose snippets by color: aeonium rosettes for greens, purples, and burgundy; *Crassula capitella* 'Campfire' for orange foliage in fall and winter; and *Senecio mandraliscae* stems for icy blue foliage.

SLEEK AND MODERN

Succulents can be used to create various looks, depending on how you arrange them and on the vases you select. For this bouquet, the designer filled an angular, snow-white vase with a single rosette of *Echeveria agavoides* 'Lipstick'; a *Crassula ovata* 'Ogre Ears' cluster; and sprigs of *Sedum* x *rubrotinctum* (pork and beans). Trailing, thin-stemmed *Rhipsalis sulcata* and string of pearls *(Senecio rowleyanus)* spill over the vase sides. A single *Tillandsia* fans out its threadlike foliage on top.

DESIGN JODI SHAW, FLOURISH—SUCCULENT FLORAL DESIGN

Add Height
Wire a delicate *Tillandsia* to a small bamboo skewer. Insert into the vase.

Tuck in Accents
These are dried slivers of a palm seed pod.

Set in Succulents
Place sprigs of trailing plants in the vase. Then add rosettes.

Add Succulents

Keep them small. Pictured: *Echeveria* and aeonium in the vase (below), sempervivum (at left), and *Echeveria nodulosa* (at right).

Choose a Vase

These mercury glass vases are 3 to 5 inches tall; fill them with cactus mix to within 1 inch of the rim.

Finish with Mulch and Moss
Cover the soil and pot rim with a collar of soft moss.

RUSTIC CHIC

For a quick arrangement to dress a table for a party, or to give as a hostess gift, fill a small, pretty vase (or several) with small succulent cuttings. Or set tiny rooted plants in soil-filled vessels, like the ones pictured here.

DESIGN **DIG GARDENS**

CLASSIC AND BLOWSY

Rounded bouquets filled with roses have a sweet, romantic look. Succulents lend themselves to that look as well, especially in a pretty vase. For this bouquet, the designer chose a *lassi* cup from India, about 7 inches high, etched by hand into brass and silver. She used succulent rosettes for the "cabbage rose" effect, then filled in around them with chocolate cosmos and greenery, including coral bells *(Heuchera)*, hop bush *(Dodonaea)*, *Leucadendron*, and tea tree *(Leptospermum)*. Delicate *Tillandsia* complete the soft effect.

DESIGN CAITLIN ATKINSON

1

Materials & Tools

18-inch-long piece of
20-gauge floral wire for
each succulent or *Tillandsia*

Wire cutters

8 to 10 succulent cuttings

3 to 5 *Tillandsia*

Pint-size glass or vessel

Flowers of choice

Floral scissors

Snippets of greenery

2

1. Wire the Succulents

Insert a piece of floral wire halfway through each succulent stem. Bend the ends downward, then twist together.

2. Wire the *Tillandsia*

Wrap one end of the wire around the base of each plant. Bend the other downward to make a stem.

3. Arrange the Bouquet

Tuck in the succulents first,
spreading evenly, then
add greenery and flowers
in the spaces between them.
Add *Tillandsia* as accents.

WEDDING ARRANGEMENTS

THE BEAUTY OF SUCCULENTS for bouquets is that they never die. That's why many talented designers use succulents instead of (or with) cut flowers to make bouquets, wedding favors, boutonnieres, cake decorations, and hair ornaments for one simple reason: The plants will live on as reminders of this special occasion. Several years ago, Marialuisa Kaprielian—a floral designer whose business, Urban-Succulents, is based in Southern California—showed me some of the special techniques she developed for incorporating succulent cuttings in beautiful decorations for a wedding. Her designs are featured here.

BOUQUET

This stunning bridal bouquet features 25 succulent cuttings, mostly echeverias with a few *Graptopetalum* and *Crassula* tucked in here and there. After the wedding, remove the tape and wire from the bouquet, then place the cuttings in a tray filled with cactus mix. While the honeymoon is in progress, the succulents will be developing roots. For a living reminder of the special event, plant a garden (or a container) and watch it grow through the years, along with the marriage.

Lengthen Stems

Attach an 18-inch piece of
20-gauge wire to each stem.

Wrap It All Up

Gather the stems together,
and wrap with floral tape
(technique, page 138). Finish
with decorative ribbon.

Add Pops of Color

Cut snippets of blooming
Kalanchoe blossfeldiana hybrids,
from purchased 2- to 4-inch pots;
wrap the stems with wire to
lengthen them.

Finish the Top

Set 2 or 3 rosettes on top of the cake, tilting them slightly to face outward.

Start Low

Working upward in a loose spiral, insert succulent stems, lengthened by wire (see technique on page 138), into the cake.

Vary Sizes and Add Color

Mix small rosettes and kalanchoe flowers between larger echeverias.

HAIR ORNAMENT

RIGHT Instead of flowers, try succulents to embellish a veil or some upswept curls. Here, three small echeveria rosettes and a tiny bunch of kalanchoe blooms decorate the comb in this bride's hair. Stems are secured to a plain hair comb with light-gauge wire. Ribbon camouflages the wire.

CAKE GARLAND

OPPOSITE *Echeveria* rosettes in various sizes encircle this tiered wedding cake like a garland. The stem of each rosette is wrapped with light-gauge wire, which secures the succulent into the cake. The bouquet on top just rests there. Before wiring and placing rosettes, allow their cut stem ends to heal (callus) for a few days. Remove succulents from the cake before cutting it.

BOUTONNIERE

No wedding is complete without a mini bouquet for the groom's lapel. Choose tiny succulent cuttings and snippets of companion plants in the same color palette as the bridal bouquet (*Echeveria, Kalanchoe tubiflora,* and *K. blossfeldiana* flowers were used here). Extend the stems with wire as shown. Then, following the steps below, make a boutonniere in minutes.

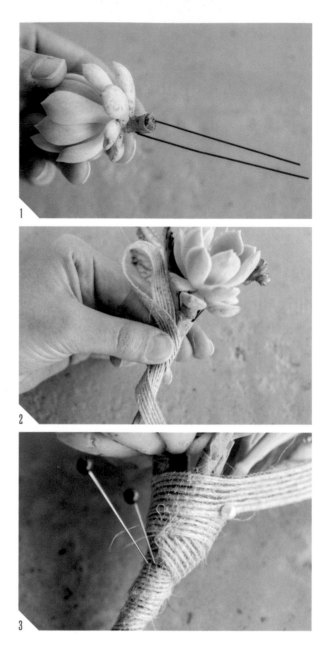

Materials & Tools

Five 6-inch pieces 20-gauge floral wire

Wire cutters

4 succulent cuttings

1 sprig of kalanchoe blooms

Floral tape

Ribbon

Scissors for cutting ribbon and tape

3 floral pins: 1 white topped, 2 black topped

1. Wire Stems

Insert floral wire about halfway through each succulent stem, close to the base of a rosette. Bend the two halves, then twist together. Repeat with a flower sprig. Gather all stems and wrap them together with floral tape.

2. Add Ribbon

Starting just beneath the bouquet, make a loop with one end of the ribbon, then wind the free end down the length of the stems and back up.

3. Pin and Wear

Insert the white-topped pin near the top to hold the ribbon in place, and the 2 black-topped pins for securing the boutonniere to the lapel.

TABLE DRESSINGS

DURING THE WINTER HOLIDAYS at Succulent Gardens, I grew and sold many wreaths for display on doors, gates, and other vertical settings. I displayed them at home as well. My wife placed our wreath on a bed of decorative pebbles, pressed into the wreath five or six small candles—secured in cake candleholders—and then placed it in the middle of our dining table.

The table receives little sunlight, so after a week or so, the plants would begin to stretch as they reached for additional sunlight, and purples and reds would fade. We didn't worry about the plants, because we knew we could gradually move the wreath to a sunnier spot, the color would return, and the plants would begin growing normally again. But the tabletop succulent arrangements pictured here should look fresh for days, or even weeks.

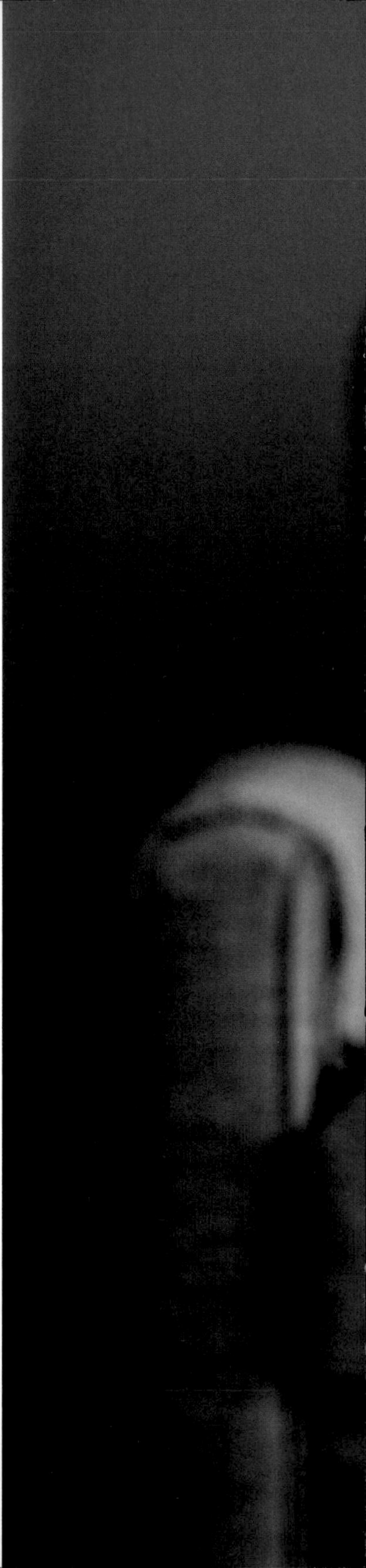

A LIVING TREE

Succulent rosettes of various sizes and shades of green give this tabletop Christmas tree its color and texture. But the tree is "green" in more ways than one. After the holidays, you can reuse or plant the cuttings in containers or in the ground. They will grow and can then provide many more cuttings for future decorations. Set the tree on a tray, to protect the table from water marks.

DESIGN CAITLIN ATKINSON

Start with a Cone

A polystyrene foam cone, about 15 inches high by 5 inches wide at the base, serves as the foundation.

Fill In

Add individual cuttings such as *Aeonium* 'Kiwi' to fill holes and enhance the design. Wire the cuttings as shown on page 138.

Use Succulent "Tiles"

Wrap the cone with 10-by-20-inch succulent "tiles" (see page 161), cutting as needed to fit the shape.

Create a Centerpiece

For variety, set one or two large rosettes among smaller sedums in each box or vase.

Dress the Plates

Succulent-embellished twigs are great take-home gifts for guests. To make them, see the details on page 144.

Add Glow
Place candles in small glass jars among the succulent bouquets.

TIP
Harvest clippings from your own plants, each with at least 3 inches of stem attached. Allow the stems to callus (heal) for several days before inserting them into the soil inside the pots.

TABLE SETTING

Succulent cuttings fill rustic square wooden boxes that together create a miniature garden on this festive table. The 10 identical boxes, each about 4 inches in diameter and made of reclaimed cedar, are arranged in offset groupings atop a bamboo table runner, with four boxes in the center, three on each side. Favors at each place setting, also made of natural materials, complement the garden theme.

DESIGN **CAITLIN ATKINSON**

PLACE SETTING

A twig, a little forest moss, a few succulents, and some glue are all that's needed to make this natural party favor for your guests to enjoy, then take home as a memory of a special evening. A day or two before assembling these favors, take three succulent cuttings per table setting from plants in your garden, so the cut ends are dry and glue will stick. Or, glue the moss in place but use fine copper wire to secure the succulents with a bit of stem to the twigs, so they can be easily removed, then rooted and planted later.

DESIGN CAITLIN ATKINSON

Materials & Tools

Assorted branches, each 6 to 7 inches long

3 small succulent cuttings per place setting

Floral adhesive, such as Tilly Tacker

Hair clip

1 small bag of moss

1. Apply Glue

Dab floral adhesive onto each branch where you want to put a rosette. Let it set for 5 to 10 minutes. Push the base of the cutting into the glue.

2. Secure the Rosette

Use the hair clip to hold the rosette in place until the adhesive dries.

3. Add Moss

Glue patches of moss along the branch.

GIFTS AND GIFT TOPPERS

PEOPLE OF ALL AGES and gardening skill levels find succulents fun and engaging. That's why these jewel-like plants make great gifts, whether you tuck a single cutting beneath ribbon to serve as a bow on a package or you drop the succulent into a pretty bag to give as a gift. After all, succulents keep on giving, and living. Once you gift them to friends or family members, you might also be gifting them a new hobby and possibly a path to succulent mania.

My wife often picks her roses to arrange in pretty bouquets that she can present as gifts. I do the same with succulent cuttings, knowing that they'll outlast the roses and continue to grow for years.

There are many ways to package succulents. Here are a few ideas, but don't stop here: Get creative.

SUCCULENT "BOWS"

Echeveria rosettes and cuttings of various other succulents—all in soft hues of jade green, silver blue, pale orange, and caramel—give these plain or patterned package wraps a natural, organic look. Some of the succulents are tucked beneath "ribbons" of twine or jute; others are glued in place. Either way, these succulents are like bonus gifts; the recipients can plant the cuttings and get them growing.

DESIGN CAITLIN ATKINSON

Kalanchoe
orgyalis leaf

Crassula
marnieriana

Kalanchoe
orgyalis

Echeveria hybrid
with Oscularia
deltoides
underneath

Sedum nussbaumerianum
with Aptenia cordifolia and
Rhipsalis

Sprig of
Rhipsalis

Sedeveria
hybrid

Echeveria pulidonis

Sempervivum hybrid

With
Love

Haworthia

Plant Succulents

Working from back to front, use tweezers to position small rooted succulents from 2-inch pots. Plants shown: stonelike *Lithops* and sea green haworthia, front, with fishhooks *(Senecio radicans)*, which resembles kelp.

Position a Rock

Settle a large rock in the sand. Pictured: white aragonite crystal *(paxtongate.com)*.

Add Sand

Pour in washed aquarium or horticultural sand from a bag with a small opening.

Finish

Using a spoon, add more sand to cover up any soil around the plants. Dust any loose sand from leaves with a soft paintbrush. Place a small rock in front.

UNDERSEA GARDEN IN GLASS

A small garden in glass makes a great gift for a special friend, to display on an indoor table. You can use any glass terrarium, but I like this Open Oval Terrarium *(shopterrain.com)* for its fresh, contemporary look. A modern take on the old "ship in the bottle" idea, it's filled with succulents that mimic sea life basking on a bed of sand. This terrarium is open on both ends and measures 6 inches long and 3¾ inches high. Wipe the glass clean with a damp cloth before planting. Water the plants sparingly; *Lithops* does not like water in winter. Display in bright light, away from a window that gets full, hot sun.

DESIGN CAITLIN ATKINSON

GIFT BAG

When dinner at a friend's home calls for bringing a little something, succulents make perfect gifts. Unlike a bouquet of flowers, a petite potted succulent won't need to be rushed into a water-filled vase as soon as you arrive. The right rosette, like the star-shaped *Gasteria* pictured, will shine in a wrapping such as this. All you do is embellish a ready-made "treat bag" *(papersource.com)*. At 4¾ inches wide and 6½ inches tall, it's just the right size to hold a 4-inch potted succulent. Look for paper netting at art supply stores.

DESIGN **CAITLIN ATKINSON**

Materials & Tools

4¾-by-6½-inch treat bag	Gift tag
Paper netting	Pen
Scissors	String
4-inch potted succulent	Small plastic clip

1

2

1. Prep the Bag

Fold the bag in half, then open and stand it up. Bend the top edge toward the exterior and fold down about ½ inch. Crease the fold flat. Repeat twice to make the bag 4 inches tall—just enough to conceal the pot.

2. Add Netting

Cut a piece of netting as tall and wide as the bag, plus about 1½ inches on each end to overlap at the back of the bag. Wrap the netting around the bag from front to back, overlapping the back ends; tuck the top edges under the bag's top folds as shown, to secure them in place.

3. Finish the Gift

Fill out the card, add a string bow, and attach the card to the bag with the clip. Set the succulent inside the bag.

FOUND OBJECTS

FEW PLANTS CAN GIVE OLD ITEMS the fresh new look that succulents can. Window shutters that are no longer needed to shade a home can be converted into a frame for showing off succulents on a patio wall. Old cowboy boots with the toe cut out look pretty cool sitting on the front porch of a ranch-style house with succulents growing out of the toes. I have planted rusty wheelbarrows with gorgeous rosettes to create movable gardens that I could wheel to various display areas. At Flora Grubb Gardens, a store in San Francisco, designers planted an old broken-down truck with succulents, for display on the showroom floor.

There are so many examples of using succulents with repurposed items that I could fill several books with the photos. A few of my favorites are pictured here.

PLOWED UP

Salvaged plow disks from an old farm tractor provide shallow bowls for planting—and a rustic-modern look for this trio of raised planters. Tall succulents enhance the mostly low plantings. They include orange-tinged *Euphorbia tirucalli* 'Sticks on Fire', which rises behind echeveria rosettes (*E. gibbiflora* 'Carunculata' and *E.* 'Morning Glow' in foreground), and *Kalanchoe luciae* in the bowl at left. Delicate mounds of chartreuse *Sedum rupestre* 'Angelina' soften the foreground of both plantings. Gravel tops the mounded soil in all planters.

DESIGN DIG GARDENS

Keep It Simple

Three kinds of plants fill each disk: a low sedum, front; a showy rosette, center; and a tall accent, like this kalanchoe, behind.

Provide Drainage

Holes in the disk bottoms fit over the pipes' tops, allowing excess irrigation water to trickle into the garden bed.

Raise the Bar

Pipes of rusted metal support the planter bowls at various heights.

Gather Succulents

Snip small succulents, such
as sempervivum rosettes and
watch chain (*Crassula
muscosa*), pictured, from
garden plants. Allow cut
ends to heal for several days.

Build a Bouquet

Gather stems of 2 or 3
succulents and wrap them
together with floral wire.

Insert in Stone

Set the bouquet in the hole
so it is just above the rim.

TIP

It is illegal to collect any natural flotsam on state beaches. So if you can't find a rock with a natural hole, buy a small, soft rock such as sandstone at a stone yard. Wet it down, then drill a hole in it, using a diamond drill bit.

HOLY ROCKS!

My favorite time of year to comb the beach near my home for interesting objects is during winter, after lashing waves have carried away much of the sand to expose interesting rocks and shells. That's where I found these smooth beauties, all with sculpted holes. Most likely, their holes were scoured out by clamlike marine mollusks, called piddocks, which use the sharp ridges on their shells to carve hiding places where they then live, protected.

The rocks make shapely natural vases for succulent cuttings. For rocks with small holes, snip an *Echeveria secunda* or *Sempervivum* 'Director Jacobs', and set the stem into the hole. Larger holes can be planted with rooted succulents from 2-inch containers.

Over the years I have been referred to as "Rockin' Robin," but I don't think anyone who used the nickname knew about my interest in rock collecting.

DESIGN CAITLIN ATKINSON

NATURE'S ART

Whenever I walk along the beach after a storm, I find shapely pieces of sun-bleached driftwood basking in the sand among tangles of seaweed. Worn smooth by waves and months of bobbing in ocean currents, many of my finds are so shapely that they are works of art, worthy of embellishing (with cactus or succulents, of course) for display on the wall. Three narrow-leafed *Rhipsalis* plants and two rosette-forming haworthia, all from 2-inch pots, embellish this piece. Before attaching succulents, clean the wood of any dirt or sand using a stiff brush.

DESIGN CAITLIN ATKINSON

Materials & Tools

5 cactus or succulents in 2-inch pots

1 small bag sphagnum moss

Monofilament

Driftwood

18-gauge floral wire

Wire cutters

1. Prep the Plants

Remove each plant from its pot and shake off loose soil. Tightly pack the moss, premoistened in water, over the soil and roots. Secure the moss by wrapping with monofilament; tie off with a double knot. Repeat with the remaining plants (or combine multiple plants in one moss ball).

2. Attach the Plants

With the driftwood laid flat, position each succulent in a curve or joint so it faces outward. Secure the moss ball to the driftwood with wire, twisting the ends together as shown. Tuck the wire ends to the back of the driftwood branch.

TIP

Driftwood from the ocean contains salts and must be cured by soaking in water (and changing it often) for 2 weeks before you attach succulents to it. Or use grapevine or manzanita prunings.

3. Water the Plants

Use one of two methods as needed: Detach succulents from the driftwood and submerge the moss balls in a water-filled tub or sink. Or submerge the entire sculpture once or twice a week (keep in mind that wire eventually will rust).

GARDEN ART

EARLY IN MY NURSERY CAREER, while riding my bicycle through small beachside communities, I began to notice many pretty succulent gardens thriving in confined spaces. One day I spotted a fruit box, beautifully planted and bursting with assorted succulents. As I stopped to study it, what flashed through my mind was an image of a box mounted on a wall like a work of art. That fruit box inspired my "living pictures," which made their debut in *Sunset* magazine in 1984, in an article titled "Frame It, Plant It, Hang It" (see page 9).

Now, a new generation of wall-hanging planter boxes—shaped like hearts, stars, states, and letters—have become readily available in stores and at craft fairs. Here are three fun ideas to get you started.

TIP

Irrigate about once a week. Remove each planted shutter from the wall, and use a watering can with a long, narrow spout. Let it drain, then rehang the shutter.

SHUTTERED SUCCULENTS

Eight colorful shutters of varied shapes and sizes, all from Building REsources in San Francisco, serve as both display racks and frames for assorted small succulents. Nestled together, they bring roomlike appeal to a dramatically dark wall. Tiny succulent rosettes, including *Echeveria* 'Imbricata' and *E. secunda*, and trailers, such as *Sedum acre*, *S. rupestre* 'Angelina', and *S. spathulifolium* 'Cape Blanco', peek out from the openings between the slats. Their roots grow into soil-filled boxes attached to the backs of the shutters. Each box, built to fit a shutter, has a hook on the back for easy removal and drainage holes on the bottom.

DESIGN LILA B. DESIGN

Prep the Shutters

Attach sturdy wooden boxes, each 2 inches deep, to the backs of the shutters. Tilt the shutters slightly upward so soil will not spill out.

Add Soil

Lay each shutter-box flat. Use a trowel or funnel to pour in cactus mix until the box is almost full. Gently jostle the box to settle the mix evenly.

Tuck in Plants

Unpot succulents and slip the rootballs through the slats (divide into smaller pieces as needed). Make sure the roots fully enter the box. Then slip in cuttings so the stems penetrate the soil. Keep the box flat for 1 week or more for rooting to start.

Modern Box

Inspired by Bauhaus modernism, this bold and blocky birdhouse has a living wall, embellished with succulent tiles.

"Eichler" Birdhouse

Like Northern California's most iconic 1950s homes, this birdhouse has a slanted roof. It's topped with a panel that holds a sedum "tile," removable for watering.

SUCCULENT "TILE"

RIGHT The "tiles," created for the rooftop gardening business, are now sold by succulent specialists and at some big box stores for garden projects. Each tile is made up of about 10 sedum varieties, all growing on a 1-inch-thick mat of coir (coconut fiber). Some companies sell several sedum mixes, including cold-hardy or colorful types, and those that do well in light shade. Remove the coir mat from the nursery tray, then use scissors or a serrated knife to cut the tile into different shapes and sizes. The sedums will continue to grow on the coir, but will grow better when placed directly on a 2- to 3-inch bed of cactus mix.

BIRDHOUSES

OPPOSITE Like us, birds need a place to call home, at least during the nesting season. Woodpeckers prefer holes in trees; bluebirds, special boxes mounted on poles. For birds that simply groove on style, Doug Barnhard, an architect and cabinetmaker in Santa Cruz, California, designs modern birdhouses with "sustainable" living walls and roofs. Two of his designs are pictured here. These houses are made of wood, which naturally insulates birds during hot days. Succulent tiles accent both.

DESIGN DOUG BARNHARD

CALIFORNIA!

A customer in Texas asked Brian Merrell to design a container in the shape of the Lone Star State. After that, he produced California and several other states. Here's how to plant your own Golden State, using succulents and a California planter box *(sgplants.com)*. If you do not want to wait for cuttings to produce roots and grow in, start with small plants in 2- to 3-inch pots as pictured.

DESIGN **BRIAN MERRELL**

Materials & Tools

1 small bag sphagnum moss

1 California planter box, about 4 inches across by 15 inches long

20 small succulents, rooted in 2- or 3-inch containers

Chopstick or stick

1. Prep the Planter

Line the bottom of the box with a ½-inch layer of sphagnum moss.

2. Add Plants

Set unpotted succulents randomly in the box. Use the chopstick to pack tufts of moss between and over the rootballs and between the frame and the plants. Set the box flat and leave for 2 weeks for the roots to take hold.

SUCCULENTS

3. Hang the Box

Hang the planter on a wall that gets filtered sunlight (no direct sun). Remove and water it about once a week; allow it to drain, then rehang.

WREATHS

I WAS ONCE ASKED if I invented the succulent wreath. I did not, but I have spoken with people who were making them in Capitola, California, in the 1950s. Small sedums and succulent rosettes are ideal for embellishing living wreaths, which bring color and beauty to front doors, patios, and tabletops.

Check out the ideas on these pages, or use your imagination to develop other wreaths using succulents. As a project, wreaths are tough to beat. The process can be fun, but also takes time, patience, and effort. People I know like to gather friends at someone's home, pool their plants and materials, and make wreaths together, often for a school or church fundraiser. They gather supple twigs, snippets of greenery and flowers, and succulent cuttings, then let the creativity flow!

TWIG WREATH

As any gardener knows, twiggy prunings are abundant at certain times of year. Instead of tossing them out, you can put them to good use as wreath frames for succulents. The wreath pictured here uses *Echeveria* 'Black Prince', *E. colorata, E.* 'Benitsukasa', and *E. pulidonis; Pachyphytum compactum; Oscularia deltoides;* and *Sempervivum arachnoideum* and sempervivum hybrids. Make sure the stem ends of the cuttings have healed before attaching to the wreath frame. Display the wreath in a lightly shaded area, away from hot sun. It should last several weeks with little care.

DESIGN CAITLIN ATKINSON

Make the Frame

Gather 10 to 12 thin prunings such as willow or grapevine, each 10 to 14 inches long. Bend them together to form a circle, then wire or tie them in place.

Hang It

After the cuttings' adhesive dries, hang the wreath by attaching a loop of wire or string, then setting it over a tack or picture frame hook.

Add Succulents

Insert the largest cuttings in crevices between the prunings and attach them with floral adhesive, then place smaller succulents between them.

Attach the Greenery

Set a 20-inch wire frame flat on a table. Position the greenery so it faces the same direction. Using a roll of 20-gauge floral wire, wrap and secure each sprig to the frame.

Add Succulents

Insert a 12-inch length of wire halfway through each succulent stem. Fold the wire downward and twist it to make a "stem." Tuck the wire through the greenery and attach to the frame.

Hang It

Mount the wreath on a picture frame hook, with the largest accents at the bottom.

TIP

Harvest greenery from your own garden to use for your wreath base. Other evergreen choices that hold up well for a few days include camellia, Carolina laurel cherry, citrus, and conifers.

LUSH AND LEAFY

This wreath has the look of a sumptuous, sunny-climate garden bed. Its blend of foliage in varied colors and textures is mostly Mediterranean, but with tropical touches. Making up the base are snippets of greenery from banksia and beefwood *(Casuarina);* brushlike coastal woollybush *(Adenanthos sericeus);* grevillea; and guava, along with sprigs of fragrant lavender and white statice. Succulents add bold shapes. They include rosettes of apple green *Aeonium canariense; Echeveria elegans,* and *E.* 'Violet Queen'; rose-tinged kalanchoes *(K. fedtschenkoi* and *K. tubiflora);* silvery *Pachyphytum opalina;* plump-leafed × *Sedeveria* 'Harry Butterfield'; and *Sedum clavatum* and variegated *S. spurium* 'Tricolor'. *Tillandsia* of silvery white and light green are evenly spaced accents.

DESIGN **LILA B. DESIGN**

FRESH AND UNFUSSY

For a creative take on the holidays that feels more Western than sprigs of holly do, tuck succulents into a premade olive-leaf wreath to hang over a fireplace. This wreath is embellished with rosettes: yellow variegated *Aeonium* 'Kiwi', pinkish *Echeveria* 'Perle von Nürnberg', and silvery *Graptopetalum paraguayense*. Pile more succulents in a trough for display on the mantel below, and surround it with your everyday ceramic vases.

DESIGN MIKHAEL ROMAIN

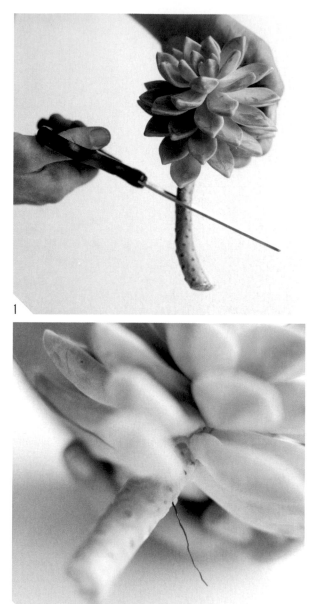

Materials & Tools

Premade olive-leaf wreath

About 7 small succulents

Floral scissors

12-inch length of 20-gauge wire for each succulent

Wire cutters

1. Trim the Succulents
Cut each stem to about 1½ inches long.

2. Insert the Wire
Push a wire through the stem of each succulent near the base.

3. Finish the Wreath

Position each succulent on the wreath, then wrap wire around to the back, twisting it to secure. For heavier specimens, tie the wire before twisting it, for more stability. Hang the wreath.

SEASONAL DECOR

NAME THE HOLIDAY and I can suggest half a dozen fun ideas for using succulents to create thematic planters and landscapes. When the San Francisco 49ers won the 1989 and 1990 Super Bowls, I supplied the San Francisco Botanical Garden with succulents that it used to create a mural depicting the team's helmet, along with the team name and the Roman numeral of each Super Bowl (XXIII and XXIV).

Succulents are so obliging, you can use them to make all kinds of holiday or party decorations. For a Fourth of July party, you might re-create the American flag in a garden bed using three kinds of succulents: *Crassula capitella* 'Red Pagoda' (red), *Sedum spathulifolium* 'Cape Blanco' (white), and *Echeveria secunda* (blue). A terra-cotta sombrero planted with succulents makes a great accent for a patio on Cinco de Mayo. Thanksgiving, Christmas, and Valentine's Day are near the top of my list for seasonal decorating, which is why I include the following projects.

THANKSGIVING: SUCCULENTS IN SQUASH

Pumpkins or squash with flat bottoms, such as kabocha or Italian stripe, can make great temporary vessels for showing off succulents. Use them to decorate a dining table for Thanksgiving or a buffet table for Halloween. When the pumpkin or squash is past its prime, repot the succulents.

DESIGN **LAUREN SMITH**

Select Plants

In the large squash, fuzzy-leafed panda plant *(Kalanchoe tomentosa)* peeks out in front of *K. fedtschenkoi* plants, whose scalloped leaf edges glow when backlit by the sunny window. In the small squash, try pink-tinged *Anacampseros rufescens* (pictured), plump-leafed *Sedum* x *rubrotinctum*, or small plants of *Crassula capitella* 'Campfire'.

Prepare the Squash

Cut off the top third. Hollow out the bottom two-thirds, leaving about 1 inch of flesh all the way around.

Trim the Squash

Use a small paring knife to cut a thin layer off the rim for clean look.

Fill the Planter

Add a small amount of cactus mix, then arrange the succulents. Fill any gaps with more soil.

Choose a Vase
Hanging glass globes and other shapes are available at garden shops and online *(paxtongate.com)*.

Insert a Plant
Bury the stem of a small rooted or cut rosette into charcoal or pumice.

Add Fill
Spoon a layer of activated charcoal or pumice into the vase.

The Design

For interest, widely space five to seven hanging vases—globes, teardrops, and other shapes—around the tree.

The Tree

Colorado blue spruce (*Picea pungens* 'Baby Blue')

CHRISTMAS ORNAMENTS

For those with a serious plant addiction, a tree hung with terrariums is reason for a "Hallelujah Chorus." A sturdy conifer branch will easily support an orb filled with a succulent or *Tillandsia* and activated charcoal or pumice.

DESIGN ANA MONFORT

VALENTINE'S DAY: EYE CANDY

Assorted small succulents in a pretty box might be the most welcome gift for that special someone who loves to garden. And it will last a lot longer than chocolates will, much as we love those melt-in-your mouth nuggets that come in heart-shaped boxes covered with red satin. This tin box (available at the Container Store) filled with succulents is easy to put together.

DESIGN JODI SHAW, FLOURISH—SUCCULENT FLORAL DESIGN

Materials & Tools

Tin box, about 8 inches long,
6¾ inches wide, and
3 inches deep

Drill and ¼-inch or ⅜-inch bit

1 small bag Excelsior moss

9 succulent rosettes in
2-inch pots

Ribbon

Twine (red and white)

Scissors

Card

1. Prep and Fill the Box

Drill holes in the box lid for air circulation. Line the bottom with moss. Place potted succulents in rows on the moss.

2. Decorate the Box

Embellish the box with ribbon and twine.

3. Add a Card

Attach a ready-made gift tag, or make one by folding a strip of construction paper, accordion style, into sections about 2½ inches square; add a photo and plant name for each plant variety in the box. On the card's back, write care tips along these lines: "Water when soil is completely dry. Place in part sun/part shade inside or out. Happy planting!"

Echeveria pulidonis x derenbergii

Sempervivum 'Emerald Rose'

Echeveria 'Perle Von Nurnberg'

Echeveria derenbergii 'Painted Lady'

Sedum pachyphyllum minor Corsican Stonecrop

CONTAINERS

IT'S NO SECRET THAT succulents thrive in containers. But to show these plants off best, you need to choose the right container—whether a tall, square vessel for the trailing stems of a *Senecio mandraliscae*; a big, globe-shaped pot for a single beefy agave; or a low bowl to fill with tiny sedums and a single echeveria. There are succulents whose foliage colors will complement bright glazed pots of candy apple red or cobalt blue, or more subtle tones of sea green, terra-cotta, silvery gray, or rust. An *Aeonium* 'Zwartkop' looks stunning in a tall container with a dark burgundy glazed finish.

Choose the pot first, in a color that matches your patio furniture, for example. Then select plants that look best with it. Or fill your nursery cart with the plants you like, and then find the pots that best complement them. If you already have a container that you want to fill with fresh plants, snap a photo of it to take to the nursery. Ask for help to find the right plants. Here and on the following pages are some examples to inspire your own container plantings.

MIXED BOWL

Rosettes of *Echeveria subrigida* 'Fire and Ice' preside over this patio planting in Seattle. Blue-green rosettes of *E. elegans, Sedum spurium* 'Dragon's Blood', and *S. hispanicum* grow around them. Tall-stemmed rosettes of *Aeonium* 'Zwartkop' rise behind. Because most of these succulents will freeze at 25°F to 30°F, the owner plants them at the end of April; they thrive in a sunny location until first frost, usually just after Thanksgiving. The container, a shallow basin 7 inches deep and 22 inches wide, is frost-proof.

DESIGN STACIE CROOKS/CROOKS GARDEN DESIGN

Add Flowers

In summer, *Echeveria subrigida* 'Fire and Ice' sends up tall pinkish stems topped with coral blooms— a lovely bonus.

Contrast Colors

Use apple green foliage, such as this *Echeveria subrigida* 'Fire and Ice', to provide cool contrast to aeonium's smoldering, reddish brown leaves.

Vary Textures

Add tiny, small-leafed sedums around the rim and tight *Echeveria elegans* rosettes just above. Textures of both help set off larger, smooth-leafed succulents.

Top
Fill the pot with soil, then plant a single echeveria rosette.

Middle
Partially fill the pot with soil, then add a 2-inch pot inside, filling it with soil. Tuck several sedum rosettes inside the rim.

Bottom
Fill a tapered glazed container, 6 to 8 inches wide, with cactus mix, to within several inches of the rim. Push a 4-inch pot inside, and add soil around it. Tuck small echeveria rosettes into the soil around the large pot.

SUCCULENT SIX-PACK

RIGHT Six small pots, gathered into a vintage wire basket, make up this simple, natural arrangement for display on an outdoor table. Each pot is filled with a different succulent—tiny gray sedums, greenish red pork and beans, red sedums, tiny gray hens and chicks. Thoughtful display is everything, says the designer.

DESIGN RYAN FORTINI

STACKED POTS

OPPOSITE Three containers, all nested together with the largest one on the bottom, bask atop a tree stump where they accent a bed of aloes and other small succulents. Filling the top pot is × *Graptoveria* 'Debbie'. Sempervivums and small aloes *(A. brevifolia)* edge the center pot, and *Echeveria elegans* studs the inside rim of the bottom pot. The planting will get better and better as the echeverias produce offsets that cascade down the sides of the pot.

CONE

When succulent floral designer Jodi Shaw discovered these "moss" cones at the San Francisco Flower Mart, she knew what she would do with them: create succulent arrangements that look like big delicious dollops of ice cream. The cones are made of hard-packed synthetic moss, so she lined them before planting. Choose small rosettes such as aeonium, echeveria, and graptoveria for the top, then tuck in a spiller such as senecio to cascade over the edge.

DESIGN JODI SHAW, FLOURISH—SUCCULENT FLORAL DESIGN

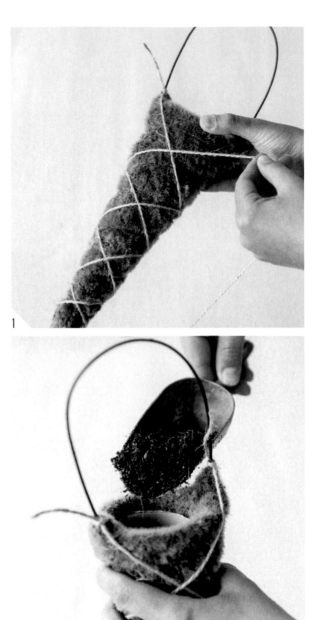

1

2

Materials & Tools

1 pressed moss cone (find at floral supply stores)

Twine

Floral scissors

Clear 6-millimeter plastic

Adhesive tape

Cactus mix

Trowel

5 small rosettes from 2-inch pots; and 1 trailing succulent

1. Wrap the Cone

Tie one end of the twine to the cone's handle. Wrap it diagonally down the cone and back up, tying off on the opposite side of the handle.

2. Add Liner and Soil

Cut and roll the plastic into a funnel slightly smaller than the cone. Overlap and tape the edges. Set the funnel inside the cone and fill it with cactus mix, pressing to firm it with each scoop.

3. Plant

Set a single rosette or several smaller succulents into the cactus mix. (If using very young succulents with few roots, push a piece of wire partway through the stems, then bend down both ends and twist together to give the plants stability so they will not topple out of the cone.) If possible, tilt or drape some plants over the cone edge, to soften the look.

With thousands of succulents available, and new ones showing up regularly at nurseries, choosing the right kinds for your garden can be challenging. To get you started, I've narrowed the field to 203 of my favorite plants, detailed on the following pages. Some form rosettes (with their leaves closely set around their centers); others trail or grow as small trees or ground-hugging mats. Many also produce offsets (young plants) that you can detach and replant—once their stems have callused (healed)—so you can grow your collection!

MY FAVORITE PLANTS

Echeveria gibbiflora hybrids (see page 218)

SUCCULENT SELECTION GUIDE

IF YOU'VE NEVER GROWN SUCCULENTS, start by consulting the lists that follow; suggested plants are arranged in categories by use. Decide where you want to plant your succulents, or the effect you want to achieve— whether a big accent beside an entry path, colorful blooms for a border, or hardy types for a cold-climate rockery. Then select the right plants from the appropriate category. Find details for your chosen plants in the encyclopedia that follows (page numbers are listed after each plant), then head to the nursery. (Succulents shown are listed in **bold**.)

BASIC LANDSCAPING

Groundcovers
Pretty to look at but don't walk on them.

Crassula capitella 'Campfire', p. 205
C. nudicaulis platyphylla, p. 206
Delosperma floribunda 'Starburst', p. 210
Graptopetalum paraguayense, p. 228
Sedum nussbaumerianum, p. 237
S. pachyphyllum, p. 238
S. x *rubrotinctum*, p. 239
S. rupestre 'Angelina', p. 239
S. rupestre 'Blue Spruce', p. 239
S. spathulifolium 'Cape Blanco', p. 239
S. s. 'Purpureum', p. 239
Senecio mandraliscae, p. 245
S. serpens, p. 245

Trailers
Plants that spill over walls.

Aloe cameronii, p. 199
Graptopetalum paraguayense, p. 228
Sedum nussbaumerianum, p. 237
Senecio jacobsenii, p. 245
S. mandraliscae, p. 245

Edgings
Succulents for growing along paths.

Aeonium pseudotabuliforme, p. 189
Aloe brevifolia, p. 200
A. x *nobilis*, p. 201
***Echeveria agavoides* 'Lipstick', p. 215**
E. elegans, p. 217
E. 'Imbricata', p. 220
E. pulidonis, p. 221
E. 'Ramillette', p. 222
E. secunda, p. 222
Sempervivum 'Commander Hay', p. 241
S. 'Director Jacobs', p. 242

Hedges
Plants for growing in rows to define garden spaces.

Aeonium pseudotabuliforme, p. 189
Agave attenuata, p. 191
A. filifera, p. 193
A. victoriae-reginae, p. 193
A. vilmoriniana, p. 195
Aloe ferox, p. 197
A. 'Hercules', p. 197
A. speciosa, p. 198
A. striatula, p. 200
Crassula tetragona, p. 205
Kalanchoe beharensis, p. 232
Portulacaria afra 'Variegata', p. 235

"Trees"
Plants for creating a treelike effect.

Aloe barberae, p. 196
A. ferox, p. 197
A. 'Hercules', p. 197
A. marlothii, p. 197
A. plicatilis, p. 198
A. speciosa, p. 198

SPECIAL SITUATIONS

Seacoast Succulents
Plants that stand up to wind and salt spray.

Aeonium canariense, p. 187
A. 'Cyclops', p. 187
A. pseudotabuliforme, p. 189
Aloe plicatilis, p. 198
Delosperma (many), p. 209
Dudleya (most), p. 211
Oscularia deltoides, p. 234
Sedum dendroideum, p. 237
S. spathulifolium 'Cape Blanco', p. 239

Cold-Hardy Succulents
Plants that tolerate temperatures at or below freezing.

Delosperma (many), p. 209
Sedum hispanicum, p. 237

Shade-Tolerant Succulents
Plants that tolerate bright indirect sunlight and afternoon shade.

Sun-Loving Succulents
Plants that thrive in full, hot sun.

Spineless Show-Offs
Gorgeous specimens that are not prickly.

Plants For Crevices
Succulents for growing between stones.

Rockeries
Succulents for growing among boulders.

Containers
Plants that have shallow roots and stay somewhat compact. Repot as they grow.

SPECIAL EFFECTS

Colorful Foliage
Succulents with leaves in luscious hues.

Showy Blooms
Plants that produce vibrant flowers.

"Undersea" Succulents
Plants resembling tidepool life.

Living Sculpture
Plants for use singly, as showy accents.

A. arboreum 'Electra'

Also known as purple pinwheel aeonium, this plant is very similar in habit to *A.* 'Jack Catlin'. It forms a low clump of four to six rosettes. Leaves are darker purple than those of 'Jack Catlin'. Flowers are bright yellow.

AEONIUM

AEONIUMS SEND UP ROSETTES of fleshy leaves in various colors, from dark purples and green to variegated with white or yellow. Beds filled with assorted aeoniums, atop stems of different heights, always make me smile; they look like giant flowers! Of the many kinds available (most native to the Canary Islands), the following represent a full range of shapes, sizes, and foliage colors.

I divide aeoniums into two types: lower-clumping varieties that reach 1½ to 2 feet tall, such as *A. canariense* or *A.* 'Kiwi', and taller (2 to 3 feet) kinds with an open branching habit, such as *A.* 'Sunburst' and *A.* 'Cyclops'. The low-growing, clumping types form mounds of tightly packed rosettes, all of similar size. *(A. canariense* is an exception; a rosette can reach up to 15 inches across, with others of various sizes tightly packed around it.) The taller varieties are more sculptural; branches are topped with rosettes 8 to 12 inches across. Both kinds work well in gardens and containers.

Aeoniums thrive near the coast where temperatures stay above 28°F, in spots that get full sun to part shade. Cool-season growers, they go dormant in summer, when they may lose leaves, then perk up once cooler, wetter weather returns in fall.

Showy flowers occur randomly on mature (2-to-3-year-old) plants; colors range from white to yellow to pink. Bees love them. After the flowers fade, the entire head dies. On most kinds, rosettes that did not bloom will take over. To encourage rebranching, clip off spent flower heads, leaving 2 to 3 inches of stem. Protect aeoniums from snails, hail, and frost. Destroy snails as soon as they appear and cover plants when freezing temperatures are predicted.

A. arboreum 'Variegata'

Tall (2 feet) with an open growth habit and 3- to 5-inch rosettes, the entire plant covers a 1½-foot diameter. Leaves are green with pronounced white edges. This plant really stands out in shady environments. White flowers appear unpredictably.

A. 'Blushing Beauty'

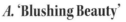

A low, clumping variety, 'Blushing Beauty' forms a full, tight mound of 6- to 8-inch rosettes. The mounding plant reaches 2 feet wide and 15 inches tall at its highest point. Leaves are green with a pronounced red or purplish tip (color varies according to plant maturity). Flowers are yellow.

A. canariense

This aeonium pumps out the largest rosettes of all the low, clumping varieties—to 15 inches across. They're biggest when protected from hot sun and watered and fed liberally. Leaves have a red edge when stressed by cold or drought. Showy flowers are white.

A. 'Cyclops'

This open, branching variety, 3 to 4 feet tall, forms big rosettes up to 8 inches across. Leaves are deep green toward the center, dark purple toward the edges. Stems below the rosettes develop lovely markings where the leaves have shriveled and dropped away. In full bloom, the plant produces spectacular bunches of yellow flowers, which add another 2 feet to the plant's height.

A. decorum

This low, clumping variety grows 15 inches tall and 2 feet wide, with rosettes about 3 inches across. Leaves are murky green to bronze. Flowers are white.

A. 'Garnet'

Similar in habit to A. 'Jack Catlin', this aeonium turns a deeper burgundy as it ages. Flowers are yellow, but unlike A. 'Jack Catlin', rosettes die after flowering.

A. haworthii

One of the most cold-tolerant of the low, clumping varieties, this one forms a mound to 1½ feet tall and 2 to 3 feet wide. Rosettes 3 to 4 inches wide have leaves of smoky gray-green. Flowers are white.

A. 'Jack Catlin'

This beauty has a low, clumping habit, with tightly packed rosettes to 6 inches across. Leaves are a rich, deep red, like Pinot Noir, and stay on the plant for most of the year. Flowers are bright yellow, and unlike most aeoniums, the rosette does not die with the flowers.

A. 'Kiwi'

The most striking of the low, clumping types, A. 'Kiwi' has green in the center of the leaves, rich yellow moving outward, and red on the edges. A clump will grow to 15 inches tall and 3 feet across, with individual rosettes 3 to 4 inches in diameter. Flowers are white, contrasting nicely with the foliage colors.

A. leucoblepharum

The plant forms a low clump about 3 feet wide and 1½ feet tall. Rosettes are 3 to 5 inches wide, with pointed leaves of bronze to almost orange. Flowers are white.

A. nobile

Growing 3 to 4 feet tall, this plant has a freely branching habit and thick, 15-inch-wide rosettes that resemble echeverias more than the typically thin leaves of aeoniums. Early forms of this plant were nonbranching and could only be propagated from seed, but most plants today are derived from a freely branching plant and are propagated from cuttings. It is one of the few aeoniums with pink-to-red flowers.

A. 'Pseudotabuliforme'

Also called green platters aeonium, this low, clumping variety produces many semi-flat-faced rosettes, each 3 to 5 inches across. The plant is striking in borders. Or plant it above a retaining wall, and it will cascade as new offsets grow out over the edge. Flowers are yellow.

A. 'Sunburst'

One of the most striking of the freely branching types, 'Sunburst' grows 2 to 3 feet tall. Rosettes are large (8 to 10 inches across). Leaves have green centers and light yellow edges, sometimes highlighted with a hint of red. Flowers are white and very showy.

A. tabuliforme

Due to its sensitivity to moisture, this aeonium is probably not the best landscape plant. It is unique as a low, nonbranching, very flat rosette (to 3 inches tall)—so flat that it is commonly called the table aeonium. Some designers use it to create water lily effects in low bowls. Flowers are white. But once they die, the whole plant dies too, and no other rosettes will appear to replace it (flowering exhausts the plant). Collect seeds to sow and grow a new crop.

A. 'Thundercloud'

This plant has the same look as *A.* 'Cyclops', but the foliage color differs. 'Thundercloud' leaves are mostly bronzy purple (leaves of 'Cyclops' are green near the stem and dark purple toward the tip). Large rosettes, 8 inches across, grow on thick stems 3 to 4 feet tall. Flowers are bright yellow.

A. undulatum

This beauty is very robust, with large green rosettes, 8 to 10 inches across, on thick, tall stems to 4 feet. It has slightly twisting leaves. For wonderful effects in garden beds, plant it behind lower-clumping aeonium varieties to provide a showy backdrop. Flowers are yellow.

A. urbicum

A large, very striking plant, to 4 feet tall, and somewhat freely branching, it often produces no branches at all. Some of the largest rosettes are up to 2 feet across. Leaves are smoky gray-green; flowers are white.

A. 'Zwartkop'

This freely branching type, to 3 feet tall, is well known for its foliage color of dark burgundy to almost black during the resting months of summer and midwinter. Bright yellow flowers contrast with the very dark leaves.

AGAVE

I LOVE AGAVES, but many of these beautiful plants, native to North America, are difficult and painful to work with. Their sharp leaf tips and shark-tooth edges require more care in handling than roses. Don't avoid them, though—agaves of any size make exquisite specimens in the garden. Just use care when handling the spiky ones.

Most agaves bloom between 7 and 30 years of age, although stress can shorten the time to flowering. When large agaves bloom, their spectacular flower stalks keep appearing over several months. Almost all agaves die after flowering, but most produce offspring, called offsets, to replace the spent plant. Removing a large specimen after the flower has died can be difficult; the task requires extra muscle and a large truck. The most widely grown agave in mild Mediterranean climates, *A. americana* (commonly called century plant) flowers only once after 20 to 30 years.

Many agaves are hardy to 25°F to 28°F, some to 20°F and below. They thrive near the cool coast or in hot inland areas in semishade to full sun. They grow mostly during summer as long as they get a little water, and they look good year-round, except during extreme drought. Older leaves become unsightly over time, so removing them in spring will allow new unscarred leaves to replace them. I also remove offsets every couple of years to keep the single specimen from looking cluttered.

Healthy agaves are seldom troubled by pests, although gophers can be a problem in some areas, nibbling on the roots and up into the body of the plant, eventually killing it. Hail can punch little craters in leaves. Cover the plant with cloth when hail is predicted. Remove damaged leaves in spring; new ones will soon appear.

Agaves—especially *A. angustifolia* 'Marginata', *A. stricta*, and *A. tequilana*—make very effective barriers when planted shoulder to shoulder; Homeland Security might take note. The sap can be caustic and cause a rash, so wear long sleeves when handling these plants to help prevent exposure.

I divide agaves into three groups: those with few spines; small to medium specimens (6 inches to 3 feet in diameter); and large specimens (4 to 12 feet in diameter). The ones I like most have attractive spines, striking leaf markings, and bold shapes.

TIP

To uproot all but the largest agaves and move them to another location, use a spade or sturdy shovel to dig a trench 12 to 15 inches deep around the rootball, and a spading fork to lift it.

MOSTLY SPINELESS AGAVES

A. attenuata

This large agave grows 6 to 8 feet tall, 8 to 10 feet in diameter. Its elegant, soft green leaves curve nicely as the leaf grows out from the main trunk. It produces yellow-green flowers in 10 to 15 years. Striking members of this clan include 'Kara's Stripes', whose leaves subtly blend hues of honey gold edged with emerald green; 'Nova' (also called 'Boutin Blue'; shown on page 185), with beautiful blue leaves; 'Super Nova', an *A. a.* 'Nova' relative that outperforms the original during the early years; and 'Variegata' (shown at right), with light gray-green leaves edged with white.

A. 'Blue Flame'

A relatively new hybrid, 'Blue Flame' grows to 3 to 5 feet in diameter and 3 to 4 feet tall. Leaves are a soft blue and very attractive. The plant produces offsets, which I prefer to remove as they appear, perhaps every other year. Flowers are yellow-green.

A. bracteosa

Growing 2 to 2½ feet wide and 1½ feet tall, this agave has narrow, light green, elegantly curved leaves. Flowers are white.

A. 'Blue Glow'

The leaves have bayonet-sharp tips; otherwise, they are spineless. They are edged with thin red bands and inner gold bands that light up when backlit by the sun. The plant grows to about 4 feet wide and 2 feet tall, and seldom produces offsets. It flowers at 10 to 12 years old. Flowers are yellow-white.

A. geminiflora

A beautiful plant that seldom produces offsets, this small agave—commonly called twin-flowered agave—grows to 3 feet wide and tall. The narrow leaves have smooth edges. Flowers are yellow.

SMALL TO MEDIUM AGAVES

A. stricta

Growing only about 1½ feet tall and wide, this little beauty forms symmetrical rosettes of stiff, bayonet-like, pale green leaves (the foliage often takes on a burgundy color when stressed). The plant does not die after flowering, but divides after bloom, eventually producing a large clump 3 to 4 feet across. Flowers are yellow.

A. 'Cream Spike'

A nicely variegated agave, 'Cream Spike' has spiky, gray-green leaves with white margins, and grows 12 to 15 inches wide, 4 to 6 inches tall. The plant forms abundant offsets; to preserve its look as an individual specimen, remove the offsets as they appear. Allowing them to mature will result in a mound of tightly packed plants.

A. filifera

This very striking, globe-shaped agave spreads to form a clump, 2 to 3 feet wide, of tight rosettes. Attractive dark green leaves, edged with white threads, make this a standout in containers and the garden. I like placing this plant in front of a south-facing rock wall where the sun will cast shadows of the leaves. The species has no spines on the leaf margins, making it a bit easier to handle than other agaves. Flowers are red.

A. parryi

This compact species has blue-green or gray-green leaves tipped with black spines, and thrives in part shade. It grows about 3 feet tall and wide, and spreads by offsets. *A. p.* 'Huachucensis' has broad, short, gray leaves tipped with brown spines. My two favorites are *A. p. truncata* and one I refer to as *A. p.* 'Castroville'; the latter, especially, resembles a giant artichoke. All bloom at 15 to 20 years of age; flowers are yellow.

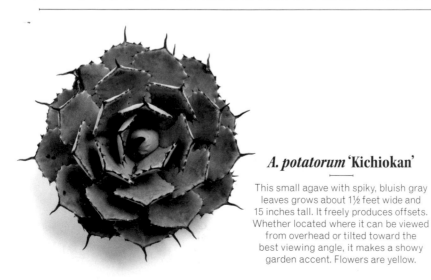

A. potatorum 'Kichiokan'

This small agave with spiky, bluish gray leaves grows about 1½ feet wide and 15 inches tall. It freely produces offsets. Whether located where it can be viewed from overhead or tilted toward the best viewing angle, it makes a showy garden accent. Flowers are yellow.

A. victoriae-reginae

The most striking of variegated agaves, this little gem grows to 1½ feet wide and 1 foot tall. The green leaves are very angular with white edges; they are spineless, except at the very tip. Red flowers appear at 10 to 15 years.

LARGE AGAVES

A. angustifolia 'Marginata'

Growing about 4 feet wide and tall, this plant forms a tidy ball of narrow, stiff leaves with sawtooth edges. As the plant ages, its short trunk (1 to 2 feet tall) becomes more visible. It blooms in 10 to 15 years (flowers are green and white).

A. desmettiana 'Variegata'

Growing 5 feet in diameter and 4 feet tall, this variety is spineless except for a spike at each leaf tip. The leaves are edged with light yellow. It performs well with morning or afternoon sun. It blooms at 10 to 12 years old; flowers are yellow.

A. franzosinii

A very large century plant that can grow 6 to 8 feet tall and 10 to 12 feet across, it has powdery grayish blue leaves with edges tipped with reddish black spikes. Spectacular yellow flowers appear in about 30 years.

A. americana

One of the most common (and most sculptural) agaves in Western landscapes, this agave grows 8 to 10 feet wide and 6 to 8 feet tall. It produces a fountain of wide leaves that grow about 6 feet long, with hooked spines along the margins and a wicked spine at the tip. (Make sure you really want this plant, and have room for it to grow, before choosing it.) Leaf color varies from dark gray-green to dark blue. At around 30 years of age, the plant produces a huge bloom stalk, 6 to 10 inches in diameter and 30 feet tall; flowers are greenish white. The plant spreads by offsets; it will grow in shady areas, but looks best in bright sun. Unlike many other agaves, this one is extremely hardy, to 10°F and colder. Several varieties are available with yellow or white stripes. *A. a.* 'Mediopicta Alba' (shown above), also called white-stripe century plant, grows 6 to 7 feet wide, 4 to 5 feet tall.

A. ovatifolia

Commonly called whale's tongue agave, this handsome plant has broad, light gray leaves about 10 inches wide that are cupped lengthwise and edged with small teeth. It grows 3 to 4 feet tall and 4 to 5 feet wide. Flowers are yellow-green.

A. salmiana ferox

Reaching 12 feet wide and 6 to 8 feet tall, this whopper has very spiky leaves, 6 to 8 feet long; give it some room to show off. Keep it shapely by pruning the offsets from the mother plant. It blooms at 20 to 25 years old; flowers are yellow.

A. vilmoriniana

Called octopus agave, it reaches 5 feet tall and 6 to 8 feet wide. The leaves are curvy, like the tentacles of an octopus, and are spineless, except at the leaf tips. The plant blooms at 7 to 10 years, sending up a bloom stalk 10 to 12 feet tall, with yellow flowers. As the flowers die, offsets appear along the stalk; they fall to the ground and put down roots.

A. tequilana

This agave, commonly called Weber's blue agave, grows about 5 feet wide and tall. Its narrow, bluish leaves, 3 to 4 feet long, are bayonet-like. In Mexico, this plant provides the basic ingredient for making tequila, but don't grow it for that reason alone; it will take you 7 to 15 years to produce your own tequila. The plant is striking, as is its variegated form. It blooms at age 7 to 10 years; flowers are green.

A. weberi

This dramatic plant grows 4 to 6 feet tall and 10 to 12 feet in diameter. The fleshy leaves are blue-gray and edged with small spines. It produces yellow flowers at 12 to 15 years of age. *A. w.* 'Arizona Star' (shown at right) is similar, but with beautiful variegated leaves of dusty green edged with light yellow.

ALOE

THESE FLESHY-LEAFED PLANTS, most from South Africa, are striking additions to the garden. They come in many wonderful shapes, from the pinwheel-like spiral aloe *(A. polyphylla),* which appears to whirl its tidy leaves toward the rosette's center, to *A. plicatilis,* whose leaf clusters spread, fanlike. Most of all, I love their flowers.

The aloes I prefer grow well in moderate coastal climates as well as inland, where temperatures range from highs in the 100s to lows in the mid-20s and, in some cases, much colder. Most need full sun, but there are exceptions. They grow mostly during the summer; all are evergreen. Their flowers generally appear between fall and spring, in colors ranging from bright orange and yellow to red and pinks, even multicolored, as with *A. speciosa.* Bloom spikes on some species create a candelabra effect above the foliage; they make striking arrangements in vases.

I divide aloes into three groups: tree aloes, which grow 3 to 6 feet tall, sometimes taller (25 to 30 feet); shrubby types 1 to 3 feet tall; and low growers (to 1 foot) that form spreading clumps 20 to 30 inches across. While most of the aloes listed are hardy to at least 25°F, frost can damage flowers; protect clusters with frost blankets.

Most aloes thrive in containers, but they develop relatively heavy root systems and can outgrow a pot within a couple of years. Repot regularly to maintain healthy plants. Snails sometimes chew on the leaves and flowers; pick and destroy them. Aloe mites can be troublesome in warmer climates like Southern California; avoid them by buying clean stock.

TREE ALOES

A. barberae

Also known as *A. bainesii,* this slow-growing aloe starts branching at about 6 feet tall. It can eventually reach 35 feet. With a stout trunk, heavy branches, and an airy canopy of narrow leaf clusters (each about 3 feet wide), it makes a massive accent for a large garden. With age, it eventually produces orange flowers.

A. 'Hercules'

True to its name, this very robust tree aloe grows faster than any others I have grown. It develops a thick trunk and branches, with broad, triangular, dark green leaves. It can reach 30 feet tall, but easily can grow 8 feet tall in 5 years from a 5-gallon nursery container. I've never seen it bloom.

A. ferox

Commonly called Cape aloe, this single-trunked tree grows to about 10 feet tall, topped with a single crown (about 5 feet across) of gray-green, red-toothed leaves. Dark orange flowers, quite large and spectacular, appear in fall.

A. marlothii

A large aloe that grows 10 feet tall and seldom branches, it forms a single head of blue to maroon leaves, studded with short spikes, 3 to 4 feet in diameter. Flowers appear in late fall and are similar to those of A. ferox.

A. speciosa

This nonbranching, single-stemmed tree aloe grows 8 to 10 feet tall; it's crowned with a big rosette of light green leaves, tinged with rose; the rosette often tilts to one side. As older leaves dry, they form a skirt that hugs the trunk very attractively. Spectacular, early-winter flowers transition from red to white with maturity.

A. plicatilis

As this plant reaches 3 to 5 feet tall (or taller with age), old leaves gradually drop, revealing a sculptural gray trunk. Thick branches are topped with fanlike clusters of long, light bluish green leaves, hence the common name, fan aloe. Orange flowers bloom on each branch in fall and spring; they attract hummingbirds.

A. vaombe

This tree aloe grows slowly to 10 feet tall in 15 to 20 years. It reaches 3 to 4 feet wide in about 4 years. Olive green leaves take on a gorgeous bronze to red hue with a few hours of daily sun. The plant flowers at 3 to 4 years of age. Red blooms are often followed by orange seedpods.

SHRUBBY TYPES

A. arborescens

Probably the most common shrubby aloe in California, it grows 8 to 10 feet tall, with branching stems that carry big clumps of light green leaves. Spiky clusters of bright orange "hot poker" flowers appear December through February. The plant is extremely durable in rugged coastal locations. It prefers dry summer conditions. It makes a good hedge. *A. a.* 'Variegata' has beautiful light green leaves with light yellowish white markings; its flowers appear a little earlier than those of *A. arborescens*. It does well in shady locations.

A. 'Blue Elf'

This dwarf hybrid with 6-inch rosettes of tooth-edged, blue-green leaves eventually forms a mound about 2 feet wide. Bright orange flowers appear through winter months.

TIP

Plant *Aloe cameronii* above a boulder used to retain a slope. Let it send offsets downward to show off against the rock's face.

A. cameronii

This is a choice plant to set out where it can cascade over a retaining wall. It is also attractive planted at the base of a large rock. When the plant is kept on the dry side, the foliage takes on a stunning orange hue. The plant grows to about 2 feet tall and 6 feet wide. Flowers are dark orange, almost red; they appear in winter, although I've seen them throughout the year.

A. ciliaris

If pruned every 3 to 4 years, this species is a medium shrub; otherwise, it behaves more like a climbing vine. The dark green foliage contrasts well with the dark orange flowers appearing toward spring. It makes a good hedge.

LOW CLUMPERS

A. distans

Commonly called jewel aloe, this plant starts as a rosette to 5 or 6 inches in diameter, then continues to grow on a stem, to 8 to 10 feet long, while running, rooting, and branching to form big clumps. Fleshy green leaves have yellow teeth along the edges. In time, stems even cascade over retaining walls or creep along the ground. Tall stems topped with tubular coral flowers, which together create the effect of a shaggy umbrella, appear in spring. Hardy to the low 20s.

A. brevifolia

This rosette-forming succulent starts out as a single plant 4 to 6 inches in diameter, then produces offsets annually that build up on one another, eventually forming a clump 2 to 3 feet across and 1 foot tall. Leaves are light bluish green with dark orange flowers appearing in mid- to late spring. It's a good choice for borders.

A. striatula

This rambling, freely branching plant grows 6 feet tall and at least 3 feet wide, with many "heads." Each is about 6 inches wide with tapered, toothed leaves and striped stem sheaths. There are two forms, one producing yellow flowers and the other orange flowers, both in the fall, and otherwise are identical.

A. 'Christmas Carol'

A Kelly Griffin hybrid, this small aloe has pointed, deep green leaves, each beautifully highlighted with dark orange-red. A single plant grows 4 to 6 inches wide, but multiple branches result in a clump 1 to 2 feet wide. Light orange flowers appear fall to winter.

A. 'Delta Lights'

Lovely green and white leaves that taper gently toward the tips give this plant its star power. It grows just 1½ feet tall and about 2 feet across. Flowers of light orange bloom in fall and winter.

A. × nobilis

Commonly called gold-tooth aloe, this little beauty forms spreading, tightly mounded clumps of pointy green leaves with toothed edges that appear distinctly gold on some varieties. Orange flowers cluster atop tall stems in summer. It makes a nice border plant and prefers dry conditions in summer.

A. polyphylla

This aloe, which forms a singular rosette to 3 feet in diameter and 2 feet tall, is known for the spectacular spiral growth pattern it develops in 5 to 7 years. Leaves are slightly translucent and light green; light orange flowers appear in fall. For a stunning effect at a garden entrance, flank the path with a pair of spiral aloes.

A. saponaria

Low, clumping rosettes grow about 1 foot wide and up to 1 foot tall. Leaves are green to rosy gray with white speckles. Bright orange flowers appear spring through early summer. Avoid planting this species next to an asphalt driveway, as I have seen offsets burrow under and erupt through the pavement.

A. × *spinosissima*

Commonly named spider aloe, this hybrid forms a very tight clump, 3 feet in diameter and to 15 inches tall. Light green leaves are toothy but soft. Orange flowers appear in late winter. It's a heavy producer of offsets and an excellent choice for borders.

A. striata

A mostly singular rosette, it grows 1½ feet wide and 15 inches tall. Leaves are light green edged with coral bands. A single plant produces two or three flower stems with orange flowers in late winter. *A. striata* × *saponaria*, a low, clumping hybrid, shows the toothy edge of *A. saponaria* and the coral edge of *A. striata*.

A. vanbalenii

Starting as a stemless rosette, it forms a low clump to 2 feet tall and about 3 feet wide. When the plant is kept on the dry side, the green leaves turn orange. Spikes of tubular orange flowers appear in late winter.

BEAUCARNEA RECURVATA

I'VE ALWAYS GROWN this plant, commonly called bottle palm. Although it is technically a perennial, it combines so well with true succulents in landscapes that it is often considered a succulent, even by professionals.

Commonly used as a houseplant, this semi-succulent has a bare, sculptural, bulbous trunk topped with branches bearing clusters of green grassy leaves at the ends. As the tree matures, it can reach 15 to 20 feet, but 6 to 8 feet is more common. It forms a living sculpture in mild-climate gardens. Give it full sun or bright light. Mature outdoor plants may bloom. Hardy to 25°F.

CALANDRINIA GRANDIFLORA

ALSO KNOWN AS *Cistanthe grandiflora*, this little beauty may not be a true succulent—it's a perennial, whose leaves are not thick and fleshy—but it looks great with my succulents. I hope more members of this family will be used in the landscape.

This plant from Chile forms a mound of blue-gray leaves that grows rapidly to 2 to 3 feet wide and 1 to 2 feet tall. Clusters of vibrant purplish, lanternlike flowers unfurl atop delicate stems, 2 to 3 feet tall, April through September in cool coastal climates, April through June in hotter locations. Prune it heavily after the bloom and watch the plant grow out nice and full. Hardy to 28°F.

COTYLEDON

COTYLEDON HAVE distinctive foliage whose form, texture, and color complement other succulents in containers and in landscapes. The bell-shaped flowers are showy and hang from flower stems, shimmering in light breezes. Most varieties are evergreen, grow 1 to 1½ feet tall and wide, and flower during summer months in their second or third year. Most handle light freezes well to about 25°F. Watch for aphids, which are attracted to flowers and tender new leaves, and keep snails at bay. Give the plants full sun.

C. orbiculata

Among the many hybrids of this plant in the marketplace, most grow 1½ to 2 feet tall and 2 to 3 feet across. This one forms a striking mounding plant. Powdery white leaves are especially attractive and also protect the plant from hot sun. Orange, bell-shaped flowers appear in the summer. *C. o. oblonga* 'Macrantha' has large emerald green leaves, 3 to 5 inches wide, with an attractive red edge and stalks of bell-shaped orange flowers.

C. undulata

This striking, 1½-foot-tall plant, commonly called silver crown, has broad, thick leaves with wavy edges and a dusting of white powder (overhead watering washes off this coating). Clusters of orange flowers appear in spring and early summer.

CRASSULA

MOST PEOPLE KNOW what jade plants are, because they're so easy to grow—you can't kill them—and they are everywhere. But there are many kinds with different growth habits, making *Crassula* a wonderful group to explore further. Some are groundcover types that creep below taller plants and cascade over the edge of a container. These South African plants thrive in Western gardens.

I group these plants into three types: medium shrub or tree forms, 2 to 5 feet tall; low, clumping types, 2 to 4 inches tall; and groundcover types. Some make striking hanging basket plants; *C. perfossa variegata* is one of my favorites. Varieties of jade plant such as *C. ovata* have been extremely underutilized over the years. Yes, they make very good container plants, but how often have you seen them used to make a hedge or border? For a jewel box effect, try *C. radicans* or *C. schmidtii*; both have low, clumping habits that are ideal for miniature gardens.

Crassula are fun to work with, especially if you like to fit smaller plants such as *C. schmidtii* and *C. radicans* into nooks, crannies, and repurposed containers, and if you enjoy shaping through pruning. All types can be pruned to create shapely sculptural plants. Snails and aphids can be troublesome. Most *Crassula* are frost-sensitive; provide protection when the temperature drops below 32°F.

MEDIUM SHRUBS OR TREES

C. arborescens undulatifolia

Sometimes sold as *C.* 'Blue Bird' and called curly leaf jade, this plant grows lower and tighter than the common jade plant. Curled leaves give it a unique texture, and its low growth habit (under 2 feet) makes it excellent as a border plant.

C. ovata

All of the *C. ovata* species grow 3 to 5 feet tall and look like shrubby trees. Leaves are generally jade green, turning red when stressed, but they vary in shape. Golden jade (*C. o.* 'Hummel's Sunset') is pretty in a pot (see photo on page 94). Or consider planting and shaping other *C. ovata* types as a hedge: *C. o.* 'ET' (shown above), with leaves shaped like E.T.'s long, skinny fingers; *C. o.* 'Hobbit', with similar but stubbier leaves; or *C. o.* 'Pacific Pink', which looks just like a traditional jade plant (so read the label!), except its flowers are pink, not white.

C. capitella 'Campfire'

This plant grows to 1 foot tall and spreads to 2 to 3 feet. Leaves are light shiny green edged with bright orange-red; like those of *C. capitella*, they turn brilliant orange as the plant matures toward fall. Tiny white flowers appear in summer.

C. tetragona

Once called princess pine, it is a treelike shrub that grows 6 feet tall and, depending on pruning, 1 to 3 feet in diameter. Leaves are light green and pointy. This plant can spread by tips breaking off and rerooting where they land.

C. capitella 'Red Pagoda'

This compact, mat-forming plant grows 2 to 3 inches tall and 15 to 18 inches wide. Leaves are green as the plant grows, then turn brilliant orangey red as growth slows. Small white flowers appear in late summer, almost exhausting the plant in the process. Prune flowers to encourage new growth.

GROUNDCOVERS

C. conjuncta

This type has stems that grow to 15 inches or more. They fall over at about 6 inches and creep on the soil. Prune regularly to encourage upright growth. The silver-gray leaves are a unique color. White flowers appear in early summer.

C. nudicaulis platyphylla

Growing about 6 inches tall, this succulent has dark green to burgundy leaves. One plant covers 1 to 1½ feet and cascades nicely over walls. A variegated pink form is a little less hardy.

C. perforata

Stems bearing green leaves grow upright until they fall over from their own weight. (The plant makes a good understory.) A variegated form has white and yellow leaves. All forms eventually cascade.

C. falcata

Often called scarlet paint brush plant or airplane plant, it grows 1 to 2 feet tall as a shrub; stake it to keep it upright. Striking gray leaves 6 to 10 inches long are propeller-shaped. In the early fall, a large cluster of scarlet flowers develops from each branch.

C. multicava

Growing 1 to 1½ feet tall, this shrub spreads to cover an area about 3 feet wide. The leaves, 2 inches in diameter, are shiny green with a pink cast. Attractive fairylike white flowers bloom in late fall. The plant responds well to severe pruning.

C. perfossa variegata

This low groundcover, 3 inches tall, has dark green leaves edged with light yellow; when mature, they are blushed with pink. White flowers appear in summer. A green, nonvariegated form has the same growth habit. Both are excellent in a hanging basket because they cascade.

CREMNOSEDUM 'LITTLE GEM'

TWO GENERA, *Cremnophila* and *Sedum,* are responsible for parenting this plant. I have worked extensively with sedums and not at all with *Cremnophila,* but the resulting hybrid is excellent in containers and the garden. This tiny jewel-like succulent has rosettes about 1 inch wide; it hugs the soil in spots that get enough sunlight, 2 to 3 hours per day. The leaves are shiny green tinged with red. Bright yellow flowers appear in late winter to early spring. Hardy to 28°F.

C. radicans

I call this tiny-leafed clumping succulent dwarf ruby for the color its leaves take on with sun and maturity. It grows 3 inches tall and 6 to 8 inches wide. Tiny white flowers appear in spring. It is an ideal plant to use between pavers and rocks in the garden and in rock and miniature gardens.

C. schmidtii

This mat-forming, spreading plant appreciates a bit of shade. It grows 3 to 4 inches tall and 6 to 8 inches wide, with long, pointy, green to burgundy leaves. Pink flowers appear in spring. It is excellent used between pavers and rocks in the garden and in rock and miniature gardens.

DASYLIRION

I USE THESE NATIVE Southwest plants to add drama and motion to a succulent garden. Their long, thin leaves shimmer in a breeze. Growing symmetrically and resembling grass, they perform well in both containers and the landscape.

Dasylirion are evergreen shrubs that grow well in a wide range of environments, handling cold, heat, and moderate coastal climates. Well-drained soil is a must; full sun is necessary in coastal locations. In hotter climates, 2 to 3 hours of direct sun will suffice; more is welcome. Most *Dasylirion* are hardy to 20°F to 25°F. *D. wheeleri* is hardy to 0°F.

Pests are generally not a problem, although these plants are sometimes attacked by scale.

D. longissimum

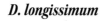

This plant grows very slowly to 15 feet tall over 15 to 20 years. Narrow green leaves, each 5 to 6 feet long, emerge from the top of the trunk, forming a uniformly globe shape 8 to 10 feet wide. The leaves shimmer in the breeze. Flowers are white.

D. wheeleri

A slow grower, *D. wheeleri* is similar to *D. longissimum,* but is shorter (6 to 10 feet) and narrower. The leaves, 3 feet long, are usually blue-green. Some forms are much bluer, though they are hard to find. Flowers are off-white to brown.

DELOSPERMA

KNOWN AS ICE PLANTS, these groundcovers from South Africa offer a spectacular range of flower colors, with new hybrids being introduced annually. They are quite versatile and they make great additions to rooftops, rock gardens, and slopes, and for cascading over walls.

There are many different members of this family to choose from. All are low-growing groundcovers that range from 2 to 12 inches tall. Foliage comes in various shades of green to light blue to gray-green and with hints of red and burgundy.

Flowers, from ½ inch to 2 inches in diameter, are very bright: yellow, red, lavender, purple, white, multicolored, and more. New varieties with unique colors are introduced regularly. The plants flower more than once in a season and hold their flowers longer than other ice plants. They thrive in sun or in light afternoon shade in hottest climates, and are hardy to about 20°F.

When healthy, *Delosperma* have few pest problems. I've seen some aphids and a little bit of snail activity. Some varieties are rapid growers and need pruning to keep them out of areas where they are not wanted. After 5 to 6 years—if the plants become thick and woody under the top growth, and the top growth is showing signs of dieback—it is probably time to remove the old plants and start new ones. Do this with cuttings from your old plants by propagating healthy tips before removing the old plants.

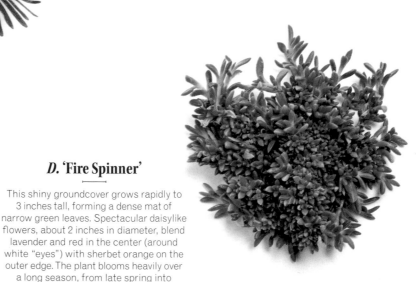

D. ashtonii 'Blut'

One of the best ice plants for cold hardiness, it thrives even above 6,000-foot elevation in New Mexico. The plant grows rapidly to about 1 inch tall and spreads to form a mat of evergreen foliage 15 to 18 inches wide. Magenta flowers appear in summer; hot, dry conditions intensify the flower color once plants are established. In hottest areas, give the plant some afternoon shade.

D. 'Fire Spinner'

This shiny groundcover grows rapidly to 3 inches tall, forming a dense mat of narrow green leaves. Spectacular daisylike flowers, about 2 inches in diameter, blend lavender and red in the center (around white "eyes") with sherbet orange on the outer edge. The plant blooms heavily over a long season, from late spring into midsummer in most climates.

D. 'Jewel of the Desert Garnet'

This plant tends to form a clump, 8 to 10 inches across and 4 to 6 inches tall. It blooms over a long period, from April through summer; flowers shaped like dandelions are intensely colored with yellow, white, and pink centers, and dark orange-red on the outer petals. Excellent in rock gardens and containers, this plant is extremely cold hardy, to minus 20°F.

D. sphalmanthioides

A very tiny variety with gray-green leaves, this plant grows to about 3 inches tall and spreads slowly. Lavender-pink flowers appear spring into early summer. The growth is very compact and makes for one of the best rock garden varieties that will nestle between rocks without growing over them.

D. floribunda 'Starburst'

Spreading rapidly, this mat-forming dark green groundcover grows to 8 inches tall and 20 inches wide. Beautiful flowers, 2 inches in diameter, have white centers; they bloom from late spring to midsummer. Tiny transparent flakes, resembling ice, cover the leaves. These plants are evergreen in warm areas. In cold-winter areas, they do best in a sheltered location with protection from frost.

TIP

Plant sweeps of several different *Delosperma* and let them grow together for a simple, attractive garden.

DUDLEYA

THIS FAMILY NATIVE to the western United States and Mexico does well in steep rocky areas of the garden where lack of water and nutrients might make conditions difficult for most other succulents. The snow-white foliage of several varieties is a standout in many gardens.

Unlike many succulents propagated from cuttings, almost all *Dudleya* are grown from seed, and a fair amount of hybridization takes place in cultivation and in the wild. This can result in some variability, and for each of the species listed here, I note the characteristics I look for.

A number of *Dudleya* have an attractive powdery coating. Touching the leaves or using oil-based fertilizer (fish emulsion, for example) removes the powder, and the plant will not look as pretty. However, the powder will eventually grow back.

Dudleya like gravelly, well-drained soil and look best when watering is not overhead. It is advisable to underfertilize, keeping in mind that a little bit goes a long way. *Dudleya* need 3 to 4 hours of sun each day. Most are hardy to 25°F to 28°F, except where noted. Aphids will attack the flowers and sometimes new leaf growth, but otherwise pests are seldom a problem.

D. brittonii

Sometimes called giant chalk dudleya, this mostly solitary, rosette-forming succulent is native to the Southern California coast. It grows about 1 foot tall and wide; leaves have a chalky white coating. In spring, stout, silvery white flower stalks arch upward. By late spring or early summer, clusters of light yellow flowers unfurl on top.

D. cymosa

This low-growing plant, 4 to 6 inches tall, has rosettes 3 to 5 inches in diameter. Foliage color ranges from bronzy green to bluish gray. Yellow, orange, or red flowers bloom in late spring and early summer.

D. hassei

This low, clumping plant, native to Santa Catalina Island off the Southern California coast, reaches 1 to 3 feet across and about 15 inches tall. Rosettes, 3 to 4 inches wide, form at the ends of bare stems; fingerlike leaves are ¼ inch thick, 2 to 4 inches long, powdery white, and reddish at the tip. Flowers are white. Hardy to 35°.

D. farinosa

A low, clumping plant that nestles well between rocks, it reaches 6 to 12 inches tall and 8 to 10 inches across. Rosettes, each about 3 inches in diameter, grow at the ends of bare stems. Leaves have distinct red tips, especially in drought, and the inner leaf can range from apple green to snow-white. Flowers are usually yellow and appear in spring.

D. pulverulenta

This Southern California native is almost identical to *D. brittonii*, except as it ages, it does not develop a stem. Reddish flowers appear in spring.

TIP

Give *Dudleya* smaller doses of fertilizer than other succulents. These plants do not need a lot of supplemental nutrients—and do not want a lot.

DYCKIA

LIKE AGAVES, these plants can be difficult to work with due to the sharp teeth on each leaf. (Wear heavy gloves when working with them.) Some very showy varieties are extremely attractive in containers and landscapes, and are well worth the difficulty in handling them.

Most of these plants produce heavy crops of offsets, ultimately forming very tight clumps. Unlike agaves, which are much more sculptural as singular specimens, *Dyckia* grow into very attractive mounding clumps, 3 to 8 feet wide. For this reason, I like to leave the clumps intact. New hybrids show up on the market regularly.

Foliage comes in spectacular colors, from silver-gray and deep purple to red and dark green. Flowers, appearing annually, are mostly yellow, orange, red, or off-white. Full sun to partial shade is the ideal exposure. In cool coastal areas, give *Dyckia* a warm spot in the garden. They are hardy to 20°F to 25°F.

D. 'Naked Lady'

So named because it lacks the nasty spines along leaf edges, this plant is easier to handle than the spiny types. Still, be careful, as the tips are sharp. The leaves are lime green, and the rosettes produce clumps 1 foot tall and 2 feet wide. Flowers are seldom seen but are yellow when they do appear.

D. 'Silver Superstar'

Individual rosettes reach a diameter of 1 foot, grow slowly, and produce fewer offsets than other *Dyckia*. Silver leaves with attractive sharp white spines and a hint of pink along the edge make this a very showy plant in the garden and in containers. Orange flowers in the summer contrast well with the foliage.

ECHEVERIA

BOTH ECHEVERIAS and sempervivums are commonly called hens and chicks, because a mother plant sends out offspring to surround her. Most kinds come from Mexico—I call them Mexican beauties. Their leaf shapes are captivating, as are their colors, which appear to radiate from inside as magically as the prisms of light from within a precious gemstone.

Echeverias seldom grow more than 15 inches tall and 1½ feet wide. A few grow as small shrubs, including *E. harmsii,* reaching 1 to 2 feet tall. Others, such as *E. gibbiflora* hybrids, grow on stalks 6 to 8 feet tall. Most are low to the ground. Individual rosettes vary in size, from 1 inch to 1½ feet in diameter.

TIP

Plant echeverias around your garden and watch the hummingbird population grow. Hummers love the nectar these blooms produce.

These plants have shallow root systems, perform well in 3 to 6 inches of soil, and thrive in the ground and containers. Many species, such as *E. elegans* and *E. secunda,* are my go-to choices for vertical gardens, since they provide excellent color contrast, and the plants remain compact over long periods.

Smaller kinds make wonderful mosaics; they come in so many foliage colors and leaf textures that you can mass, or mix and match, with spectacular results. You can create a rainbow effect by supplementing echeverias with a couple of other succulent varieties, beginning with red *E.* 'Spruce Oliver'; orange *Sedum nussbaumerianum* and yellow *S. rupestre* 'Angelina'; blue *E. secunda*; and green *E.* 'Dondo'; and finishing off with *E.* 'Purple Afterglow'.

All echeverias are evergreen. Flowers appear mostly spring, summer, and fall, on stems 2 to 3 feet tall. They come in shades of yellow, orange, or red, and sometimes blends that remind me of the candy corn I gobbled up as a kid. The flowers attract hummingbirds and bees. Many are excellent in bouquets.

Most plants grow well in coastal areas with partial to full sun. Inland, protect them from hot midday sun. For best form and color, plant them in a spot that gets 3 to 4 hours of direct sunlight per day. Most are hardy to 25°F to 28°F.

Water can collect in the centers of echeveria rosettes, glistening in sunlight like jeweled beads. To remove it, carefully swab it up with the tip of a rolled paper towel, especially if it might contain pesticide or fertilizer residue. Both can concentrate and possibly burn the new leaves.

Aphids are drawn to new echeveria flowers and tender new leaves. In cold, damp winters, the fungus botrytis can be a problem, especially where air circulation is poor. Avoid overhead watering, and cut back on fertilizer in fall to allow plants to harden off before winter. Control snails and earwigs, which chew on the beautiful leaves.

E. 'Afterglow'

This elegant hybrid, with rosettes 12 to 15 inches across, has leaves of powdery pinkish lavender edged with brighter pink; the colors are more intense in full sun, softer in partial shade. The plant grows 1 to 2 feet tall. Flowers of deep orange-red appear in summer; their stalks can emerge from below the bottom leaves or sometimes from the top of the plant (remove flower stalks to keep the plant looking tidy). A new, darker purple variety, E. 'Purple Afterglow', has the same growth habit and flower color.

E. agavoides

All types produce a 1-to-1½-foot-wide rosette about 6 inches tall. The offsets then make a very tight mound 2 to 4 feet across and 12 to 15 inches tall. Waxy leaves are 2 to 3 inches long. E. agavoides is light green. 'Red Blush' (shown above) has a green leaf with a rose blush and red flowers in spring or summer. 'Ebony' (shown on page 185) turns very dark red, almost black on the outer half of the leaf. 'Lipstick' (shown on page 184) becomes lipstick red on the outer half of the leaf.

E. 'Benitsukasa'

This plant closely resembles E. nodulosa. But there are distinct differences between the two. The purple in the leaf of E. 'Benitsukasa' is much darker than in E. nodulosa, and the growth is slower and more compact. E. 'Benitsukasa' stays low—4 to 6 inches tall—and about as wide. Flowers are orange and yellow. The plant is an excellent choice for containers.

E. 'Black Prince'

Leaves of this lovely hybrid emerge greenish, then darken to nearly black—hence the common name, black hens and chicks. Rosettes grow 3 to 4 inches across. The plant freely produces offsets, ultimately forming a mound 6 to 10 inches across. The unique foliage color makes this plant a popular choice for beds and containers. Flowers are red.

E. cante

Rosettes are 1 foot in diameter and 8 to 10 inches tall. They seldom have offsets. Foliage color varies; the most stunning foliage is powdery white with a hint of blue and a red edge. Yellow-red flowers appear on 1½-foot-tall stems in summer.

E. ciliata × nodulosa

A cross between *E. ciliata*, a species from Oaxaca, Mexico, and *E. nodulosa*, from a wide range within central Mexico, this lovely plant has rosettes 5 inches wide that freely form offsets, resulting in a nice mound 8 to 10 inches across and 3 to 4 inches tall. Leaf color can vary from light apple to dark green. Flowers, appearing in spring on 3- to 6-inch stems, are orange and yellow.

E. 'Cassyz Winter'

This plant reaches 5 to 6 inches in diameter and 2 to 3 inches above the soil, and produces offsets tightly growing around the mother plant. During the warm growing season, leaves are light off-white with a hint of blue. As winter approaches and growth slows, the leaves turn reddish orange, like a colorful sunset. Flowers are orange and yellow on an 8- to 10-inch stem shaped like a shepherd's crook.

E. colorata 'Mexican Giant'

Rosettes 10 to 12 inches freely produce offsets that grow into a very attractive mound 20 to 30 inches across. Leaves are powdery white with pointy red tips. Pinkish red flowers with a little yellow appear in spring to summer on 10- to 12-inch stems.

E. 'Contempo'

Growing 6 to 8 inches wide and 10 to 12 inches tall, this plant has soft, greenish blue leaves, edged with red, that are about 3 inches wide. Flowers of reddish orange appear on 1-foot stems from late spring into summer.

E. craigiana

The rosette grows about 8 inches wide, with powdery brownish leaves. Reddish flowers appear in summer on stems 15 to 20 inches tall. Plant seldom produces offsets.

E. 'Crinoline Ruffles'

Each rosette remains low to the ground, 3 inches tall, and about 4 inches wide. Variations range from light blue to sea green, with ruffled edges trimmed in reddish pink. Orange and yellow flowers grow on stems 6 to 8 inches tall. This is a great succulent for planting en masse.

E. 'Culibra'

This plant's silvery green leaves have wavy edges that roll themselves into tubes 1 inch wide and 3 inches long. A rangy growth habit makes it a poor choice for use in vertical gardens, but it is attractive in pots and garden beds. When it gets too rangy, prune and replant the heads. Orange flowers appear in summer.

E. derenbergii

Small rosettes to 3 inches wide produce abundant offsets to form a clump 6 to 8 inches across and 3 inches tall. In time, offsets drape over the edge of a container. Glaucous leaves are finely edged with red that looks painted on, hence the plant's common name, painted lady. Yellow flowers blushed with orange appear on 3-inch-tall stems in spring.

E. 'Domingo'

Soft blue leaves grow 4 to 6 inches long, producing a rosette about 10 inches in diameter and 4 inches tall. The leaf has an attractive light powdery coating with pink hues toward the tip. Salmon-yellow flowers appear in summer.

E. 'Dondo'

Short, tight leaves make for a very compact rosette 3 to 4 inches wide and 1 to 2 inches tall. Leaves are light dusty green and produce offsets, forming an attractive clump. Orange flowers appear in late winter to early spring. 'Dondo' is excellent in vertical plantings.

E. 'Doris Taylor'

This pretty plant produces open rosettes about 5 inches wide, with kitten-soft fuzz covering light green leaves. The plant branches to form a cluster 15 to 20 inches across. Flowers of orange-red to yellow appear on 4- to 6-inch stems in summer.

E. elegans

This is another old favorite, used in landscapes since the 1950s. The common name, Mexican snowball, refers to the country of origin and the plant's powdery whitish foliage. Rosettes grow 4 to 6 inches wide. They produce offsets freely, creating a mounding effect that's especially useful at the front of a border. Orange and yellow flowers appear in the spring on 10- to 12-inch stems.

E. GIBBIFLORA HYBRIDS

There are dozens of hybrids in this group, some with smooth-edged leaves, others with ruffled leaves. Foliage colors vary widely from light green, to red, to blue and lavender. Some have red edges. Rosettes grow to 12 inches wide on stems 5 to 8 feet long. Most produce very showy flowers ranging from yellow to orange and red on colorful stems 2 to 3 feet tall. As a stem grows longer, the rosette diameter shrinks. Remove the rosette in the spring and replant it, and it will again grow large in diameter. This plant is very showy in containers and gardens.

E. g. 'Coral Glow'

Rosettes to 8 inches diameter have leaves of soft blue with smooth, dark pink edges that light up when backlit by the sun. Coral pink flowers appear in summer.

E. g. 'Dicks Pink'

A solitary rosette, 6 to 8 inches across, grows on a 1-foot-tall plant. Light blue-green leaves with slightly wavy, light pink edges are pretty when backlit by the sun. Pink flowers appear in spring or summer.

E. g. 'Etna'

This plant has especially bumpy leaves, which appear as blisters, called carunculations. Bumps on 'Etna' resemble erupting volcanoes, thus the name, for Mount Etna, Italy's most famous volcano. Leaf edges are ruffled; rosettes grow to 8 to 10 inches in diameter. Flowers are orange and yellow.

E. g. 'Mahogany'

Leaves of deep red to mahogany make this plant a standout, especially when paired with icy blue foliage. Rosettes 10 inches wide unfurl large, open leaves 4 to 6 inches long, on stems that grow 4 to 6 inches in 2 years, then continue growing up to 6 to 8 feet in several more years. As the stem lengthens, rosettes are narrower; remove and replant them with only a 2-inch stem every 3 to 4 years. Flowers are orange and yellow, appearing in mid- to late summer on stems 2 to 2½ feet tall.

E. g. 'Morning Glow'

This plant has a very handsome rosette 10 inches wide with leaves 3 to 4 inches wide and 4 to 5 inches long. It goes through mesmerizing color transitions, from off-white in the center, to light purple, then pinky purple with a distinct red edge. Flowers are reddish orange on 15- to 20-inch stems.

TIP

For a striking effect in a garden bed, plant a row of dark-leafed *E. gibbiflora* 'Mahogany' with icy blue *Senecio serpens* in front.

E. g. 'Red Ruffles'

This is an especially showy *E. gibbiflora* hybrid with ruffled leaf edges. Rosettes are 8 to 12 inches wide. Stems grow 4 to 6 inches in 2 years and then continue growing up to 6 to 8 feet in several more years. As the stems lengthen, the rosettes become narrower. To keep the plant shapely, remove rosettes every 3 to 4 years and replant them with only 2-inch stems. Red-orange flowers, on stems 2 to 3 feet tall, appear in summer; they attract hummingbirds.

E. harmsii

This small shrub grows 10 to 12 inches tall and as wide. A velvety fuzz covers the leaves, which start out green and turn burgundy-red toward the edges. Rosettes 2 to 3 inches wide grow on stems 6 to 8 inches tall. Orange and yellow flowers appear on 3- to 4-inch stems in spring. This plant can be difficult to grow in cool coastal areas.

E. 'Imbricata'

Also known as *E. x imbricata*, this old favorite has light blue rosettes, 8 inches wide, with rosy leaf tips, on stems 4 to 6 inches long. The plant grows offsets, ultimately forming a mound 15 to 18 inches across. Replant overgrown plants every 3 to 6 years, as the lower stems turn woody. Orange-yellow flowers appear in spring on stems 8 to 10 inches tall. 'Imbricata' is excellent in borders and also thrives in semishade.

E. 'Lady Aquarius'

Rosettes grow 8 to 10 inches wide, with beautifully ruffled leaf edges. The plant produces offsets, but not prolifically. Newer leaves are light blue and powdery, with a very attractive red edge. Orange flowers appear on 10- to 12-inch stems shaped like a shepherd's crook.

E. lilacina

Silvery white leaves with a light powdery coating give this rosette-forming succulent its common name, ghost echeveria. Foliage remains silvery gray with a hint of pink throughout the year. Each rosette grows 6 to 8 inches wide and forms abundant offsets. The plant stays low to the ground, just 4 to 6 inches tall. Flowers are light orange. It is excellent as a border plant or tucked into 3- or 4-inch-wide crevices between rocks.

E. 'Lola'

Neat rosettes are similar to those of *E. elegans,* one of its parents, but are greener, with rounded leaves ending in a point, and have a hint of lavender-rose seeming to glow from within. The rosettes are only 2 to 3 inches wide and grow on stems 3 to 4 inches tall in several years. The plant looks best when set low on the soil, so prune and replant it every few years. Flowers appear in summer and are orange and yellow pastels on 2- to 3-inch stems.

E. multicaulis

This shrubby, free-branching beauty has small rosettes on bare stems 8 to 10 inches long. It's commonly called copper leaf, which refers to the bronzy copper leaves, but in my experience, the leaves are usually green with red tips. Dark orange flowers appear on 2-inch stems in spring or summer.

E. nodulosa

Known as painted echeveria, this
small, shrubby plant has rosettes 3 to
5 inches in diameter on stems 4 to
6 inches long. In the young, single rosettes,
green leaves have beautiful red markings.
As the stems grow, the markings fade
a bit. To regain the bold leaf markings,
remove and replant the rosette. Flowers
appear on 4- to 6-inch stems in summer.
A newer variety, *E.* 'Benitsukasa' (see
page 215), is very similar but maintains
better foliage color.

E. 'Orion'

Rosettes grow to about 10 inches in diameter and stay low to the ground,
about 5 inches tall. Leaves are lightly powdered and pinky lavender. Orange flowers
appear on 3- to 6-inch stems.

E. peacockii

This plant forms a 3- to 4-inch rosette of
striking powdery white to silvery blue
leaves, sometimes tipped in red, on short
stems 4 to 5 inches tall. It produces
offsets sporadically. Pink flowers appear
on 10-to-12-inch-tall stems in late spring.

E. 'Perle von Nürnberg'

Pinkish lavender leaves make this a
very popular plant. It grows 3 to 5 inches
wide and 2 to 4 inches tall. *E.* 'Purple
Pearl' has even stronger color and a more
robust growth habit.

E. pulidonis

This slow grower has stemless rosettes
4 to 6 inches in diameter, made up of
nicely incurved leaves that are green,
sometimes off-white, with a defined red
edge. The plant produces offsets heavily,
growing into an attractive mound 12 to
15 inches across. Yellow flowers appear on
8- to 10-inch stems in spring.

E. 'Ramillette'

The jade-green rosette with pointed leaves tipped in red is very similar in size and color to that of *E.* 'Dondo', but the leaves are more open. Flowers of orange and yellow appear on 2- to 3-inch stems. 'Ramillette' is excellent in vertical plantings. A handsome, crested form is also available.

E. runyonii

An 8- to 10-inch rosette with floppy leaves forms offsets freely, ultimately developing into a clump 12 to 15 inches wide and 8 to 10 inches tall. Leaves are dusty off-white. Orange and yellow flowers appear in late summer. *E. r.* 'Topsy Turvy', with uniquely curved leaves, is a popular variety.

E. 'Sagita'

This plant forms a low, stemless rosette, 6 to 8 inches wide. Leaves are a bit narrow and pointy, with dabs of red on the outer edges. 'Sagita' is pretty in containers and works well as an edging in garden borders. Try planting it in front of taller *Agave attenuata* 'Variegata'.

TIP

Echeveria 'Sagita' is great for viewing up close. Plant it singly in a glazed, caramel-colored pot with gold gravel mulch, and display on a patio table.

E. secunda

This compact beauty is wonderful to work with. Rosettes 2 to 3 inches wide and just 1 inch tall produce offsets that are tightly attached to the mother plant, which develops a clump about 6 inches across in the first year. Leaves are blue and pointy, contrasting well with the tiny orange and yellow flowers on 3-inch curved stems. *E. s.* 'Blue Mist' (shown above) has lighter bluish leaves.

E. setosa

Dense rosettes of 3 to 6 inches surround themselves with tightly held offsets, forming a mound 2 inches tall and 6 to 10 inches wide. Green leaves are covered in fine fuzz, giving the plant a frosty look. Flowers of bright red and yellow appear in summer on stems 4 to 10 inches tall.

E. shaviana

This showy succulent with short-stemmed rosettes 4 to 6 inches wide produces offsets freely to form clumps 8 to 10 inches across and 4 to 6 inches tall. Leaves are dusty light purple. Pink flowers appear in summer on 10- to 15-inch stems. My favorite of all the echeverias, this plant is elegant, with the classic shepherd's crook shape.

E. 'Spruce Oliver'

This is one of the few "stemmy" echeverias that I like, because it creates a handsome, sculptural effect. Rosettes grow to 4 inches wide on stems 8 to 10 inches tall. Leaves start out green, then turn red with maturity and several hours of direct sun. Orange and yellow flowers are lost in the bright red foliage.

E. subrigida

The solitary rosette, 6 to 10 inches wide, has curvy leaves 6 to 8 inches long. Leaves range from sea mist green to blue, with a light powder coating and distinct red edges. Pink flowers bloom in summer on strong stems 8 to 12 inches long.

E. subsessilis

This plant forms a loose clump, 8 to 12 inches across, of open-faced rosettes 6 inches wide. Lightly powdered leaves are pale blue. Pastel orange and yellow flowers appear in summer on 6- to 10-inch stems shaped like a shepherd's crook.

E. 'Violet Queen'

When producing offsets, this choice plant forms a nice clump, 12 to 15 inches across and 8 to 10 inches tall. Rosettes are 4 to 6 inches wide. Leaves are powdery with a hint of pink toward the tips with maturity. Flowers are reddish orange on weak 3- to 5-inch stems.

E. 'White Rose'

Each rosette grows to about 1 foot wide and grows offsets freely, producing a large mound to 1 foot tall. Foliage is pale blue-green. Large pink flowers appear on strong stems in summer.

ECHINOCACTUS GRUSONII

ALL CACTUS ARE technically succulents, capable of storing water in their tissues and thriving in droughts. The only difference between them and the plants that most people call succulents is this: Cactus are generally leafless. They have stems, modified into thick-skinned cylinders or pads, where they store water. Most species have spines for protection from browsing animals. Of all the gorgeous kinds available, I include this one, golden barrel, because many gardeners mix it with more traditional succulents, especially in Southwest gardens.

Native to Mexico, golden barrel is prized for its rounded shape with prominent ribs and stout spines. It nearly glows when backlit by the sun. It grows slowly to 4 feet tall and 2½ feet in diameter; with age, it often produces offsets to form clumps 6 feet across. Showy yellow flowers appear on top of the barrels in summer.

For spectacular effects in dry gardens, cluster these cactus in front of boulders or widely space them with decomposed granite mulch around them to set them off (see photo on page 88). When handling these spiny critters, I wad up newspaper and use it like cushioned pads on each side of the plant. The paper absorbs the spines, allowing me to lift the plant without getting poked and also protecting the beautiful spines from breaking.

Golden barrel grows best in full sun and needs water every couple of weeks in summer. Protect it from hard winter frosts to prevent scarring.

To keep it clean of leaves, dust, and other wind-blown debris, some gardeners use a whisk broom, passing it gently over the plant's top.

EUPHORBIA

IN THE RIGHT SETTING, each of the following is unique and dramatic. But beware: Most have poisonous white sap that bleeds from damaged leaves or stems, so wear gloves and goggles when handling.

Most euphorbias originate from South Africa, are frost-sensitive, and require good drainage. Some have cactuslike spines, and most have few, if any, leaves. Others, like *E. milii*, have showy flowers. All make excellent container plants, and most love hot weather, but not necessarily full all-day sun. Most are hardy to 25°F or 28°F.

E. caput-medusae

This plant sends out bumpy, snakelike green branches from a central tap-rooted caudex (a thickened, rooted stem), to 10 to 15 inches long or more. The plant stays about 1 foot tall. White flowers appear in late spring and early summer. I once planted this species in a container shaped like a woman's head—like Medusa from Greek mythology, daughter of sea god Phorcys, who had serpents for hair.

E. ammak variegata

This very sculptural, columnar euphorbia grows 6 to 8 inches wide and 10 to 15 feet tall, eventually branching openly. The column is marbled white and green, with a hint of red when stressed. Four vertical ribs are studded on the margins with reddish brown spines that add contrast. The plant makes a bold, sculptural presence in the landscape. Pale yellow flowers appear throughout the year.

E. flanaganii

Similar to *E. caput-medusae,* this euphorbia has thinner branches 4 to 6 inches long. It is prostrate, like a flattened rosette, with fingerlike leaves upturned at the ends. Tiny pale yellow blooms appear in the center of the plant in summer.

E. ingens

In its native South Africa, this columnar euphorbia forms a tree 30 to 40 feet tall. In cooler climates, it grows very slowly. A friend once told me these plants kind of sit there unless the temperature soars to 100°F or more, which causes rapid growth. Very similar to *E. ammak variegata*, it has green, upright columns that make a bold, sculptural statement in the landscape.

E. mammillaris

This freely branching euphorbia reaches 8 to 10 inches tall. When grown in full sun from a young age, plants are tightly branched, forming dense mounds. Those in partial shade are more open branching and treelike. *E. m.* 'Variegata' has very thin branches.

E. milii

This freely branching shrub reaches 5 to 6 feet tall or more in warm climates. Many hybrids have flowers of different colors. They are quite cold-sensitive, but some tolerate a light freeze. They make great container plants in warm, sunny locations and produce flowers year-round. Keep dry in winter; all the leaves will drop, but flowers will continue to appear.

E. pseudocactus 'Zig Zag'

This plant has beautiful markings along the stem and a zigzag growth pattern. It grows upright to about 4 feet tall, branching freely to form a candelabra shape over time. When cut, it bleeds a poisonous white sap. Yellow flowers appear in spring. Hardy to 32°F.

FAUCARIA TUBERCULOSA

NATIVE TO THE WESTERN UNITED STATES and Mexico, this family does well in steep rocky areas of the garden where lack of water and nutrients might make conditions difficult for most other succulents. The snow-white foliage of several varieties is a standout in many gardens.

Leaves of this succulent are studded with bumpy growths, called tubercles, that give the plant an oddly interesting look. The plant grows to a diameter of 2 inches and forms a slightly mounded clump 6 to 10 inches across and 3 to 4 inches tall. Bright yellow flowers appear in fall, each large enough to cover the entire plant. The plants are small and easy to maintain in containers. But they can get lost in the landscape; place them where they can be easily viewed, such as at the front of a border, and protect them from more aggressive-growing plants nearby. Hardy to 25°F.

GASTERIA MACULATA

THIS SCULPTURAL PLANT is closely related to aloes. Like aloes, its flowers attract hummingbirds. Swordlike leaves grow upright from the soil, resembling garden trowels fanned out in a basket. A low grower just 6 inches tall and 8 inches wide, it produces offsets freely to form a tightly packed clump 12 to 15 inches across and 10 to 12 inches tall. Bladelike leaves grow 6 to 8 inches long. Deep green in shady locations, they develop orange coloring in hot sun or when stressed. Flowers of salmon to green appear in spring on 3- to 5-foot stems. Hardy to 30°F.

GLOTTIPHYLLUM NELII

THIS LOW GROWER is about 2 inches tall and reaches about 5 inches wide. It looks like ready-to-eat gummy candy, with its 1-inch-thick leaves that are translucent, shiny, and lime green. They damage easily; handle with care. The plant produces offsets that form clumps 10 to 12 inches wide and 3 inches tall. Bright yellow flowers appear in the fall. Hardy to 28°F.

GRAPTOPETALUM

AS YOUNG PLANTS, these beauties are often mistaken for echeverias. But *Graptopetalum* have distinctly different, star-shaped flowers that appear on stems toward the branch tips. Some have 2-to-3-foot-long stems that creep along the ground; others are effective when cascading over a retaining wall or when dangling over the edges of hanging baskets—one of the ways I love to use them. Still others stay low and compact, producing offsets around the base to create attractive, tightly clumping mounds.

No other plant can duplicate the textural effect of these easy-to-grow succulents. Whether in coastal or hotter inland areas, these plants thrive in containers and in the landscape. Keep snails away; also watch for aphids on new flowers and leaves. Most varieties respond well to severe pruning in late spring and early summer. Prune periodically to keep them fuller. Flowers are attractive; the best candidate for bouquet quality is *G.* 'Superbum'. Most are hardy to 25°F or 28°F.

G. amethystinum

Rosettes about 3 inches wide start out low, but over time their stems grow 10 to 15 inches long, snaking over the soil or cascading from a container. Plump leaves are lightly powder coated and are soft lavender when new, turning whitish green with age. Attractive star-shaped flowers, appearing in summer, are tipped in carmine red.

G. paraguayense

This attractive groundcover has rosettes about 3 inches wide on stems 3 to 6 feet long. It's also quite handsome cascading over walls. Whitish yellow flowers with red tips appear in spring to early summer. Different variations are available, including one with pinky silvery gray leaves and another with light bluish white leaves.

G. 'Superbum'

An upright, freely branching plant, it has flat-faced rosettes, 4 to 5 inches wide, that appear to look out at you. The plant grows 2 or 3 feet tall or more. Flowers, star-shaped with red tips, grow on stems resembling those of baby's breath from winter into spring. 'Superbum' is a bit sensitive to the combination of cold and damp in winter.

SUCCULENTS

GRAPTOSEDUM 'DARLEY SUNSHINE'

STEMS OF THIS PLANT grow quite long, eventually creeping along the ground and forming mounds to about 8 inches wide. Plant it near retaining walls or the edge of a container and let it cascade. Off-white flowers appear in spring and summer. Hardy to 28°F.

TIP

Plant *Graptosedum* about 6 inches apart, center to center, for a showy groundcover. Or let it cascade down a slope to create a waterfall effect.

X GRAPTOVERIA

THESE HYBRIDS are all well suited for both containers and landscapes, offering a great diversity of form color and texture. Most display flowers resembling those of *Graptopetalum* and rosettes with mixed characteristics of echeverias and *Graptopetalum*. Give them full sun to partial shade. Most are hardy to 25°F to 28°F.

x *G.* 'Debbie'

Rosettes, each 5 to 6 inches wide, grow on semi-upright stems that lay on the sides of a container, but do not cascade over the edges like the more snaky *Graptopetalum*. Leaves are pinkish lavender, becoming off-white when older. Yellow star-shaped flowers appear in late spring to early summer.

× *G.* 'Fred Ives'

Large, open rosettes 6 to 10 inches wide grow upright on stems 2 to 4 feet long; eventually the stems lean over to the ground, even cascade, as they reach 1 to 1½ feet long. Leaves are lavender to purple. Yellow flowers bloom in summer. 'Fred Ives' is excellent in containers and landscapes.

× *G.* 'Opalina'

Very attractive moonstone-like leaves are 2 to 3 inches long and 1 inch across on a 5-to-6-inch-wide rosette. Add to this the tightly packed offsets around the mother plant, and you get a lovely 12-to-15-inch-wide mound, 10 to 12 inches tall. Leaves are soft powdery blue with light pink tones toward the tips and undersides.

× *G.* 'Silver Star'

This rosette grows 3 to 5 inches in diameter and 1 inch tall. The offsets produce a tightly packed cluster 8 to 10 inches across and about 2 inches tall. Silvery green leaves are pointed, with thin, hairlike strands on the tips.

HAWORTHIA

THESE LOW GROWERS perform well in shady areas and make excellent container plants. Because the rosettes are small and often have dark green foliage, they can get lost in a garden. Place them toward the front of a border, and keep in check any more aggressive plants growing nearby. I list only two, but there are many more to explore.

Flowers appear on thin stems and are often white; sometimes plantlets grow off the flower stem. Leaves are generally green, but surfaces of some species are banded or speckled with white. When the plant is stressed, the leaves turn orange—often a sign the plant has lost its roots. Plants will generate new roots after you remove older decayed roots, or they decay on their own.

During droughts and in areas that are kept too wet, these plants shed their roots; make sure the soil drains well. Pests are generally not much of a problem, although I have seen aphids on new flower stalks and mealybugs on stressed plants. Most haworthias are hardy to 28°F.

H. 'Big Band'

Each rosette grows to about 4 inches wide, producing offsets that tightly cluster around it. The plant reaches 6 inches tall. Leaves are dark green, with beautiful raised white bands on the backsides. Flowers are off-white on thin stems, 6 to 10 inches tall.

H. fasciata 'Superbum'

This plant is similar to *H.* 'Big Band', with striped, pointy-tipped leaves. But it forms larger rosettes, to 8 inches in diameter. Hardy to 30°F.

HESPERALOE PARVIFLORA

TECHNICALLY NOT A SUCCULENT, this sculptural plant is a great companion for succulents and cactus in Southwest-style gardens. In fact, it's native to the Southwest. Stiff leaves curve outward from the base, creating a fountain-like effect, with the leaves bobbing in the slightest breeze. The gray-green leaves, ½ inch wide and 4 to 5 feet long, have hairlike strands along the edges. The plant produces offsets and stays tightly clustered—so much so, it is difficult to see the separate offsets. It can reach 4 to 6 feet across. Reddish flower stems appear in summer, growing a foot longer than the leaves. Hardy to at least 0°F.

JOVIBARBA HEUFFELII

ALPINE SUCCULENTS from Eastern Europe, *Jovibarba* have leaves similar to those of sempervivums and the rosettes look very much the same.

Rather than sending out offsets on stems, the plants divide, producing new offsets between older leaves. Foliage comes in strong colors, from yellow and orange to red, purple, and chocolate brown. 'Blaze' has vivid green leaves brushed with deep reddish brown. 'Inferno' (shown below) has rosettes 2 to 3 inches wide; as they divide, they form attractive mounds 12 to 15 inches across and 2 to 4 inches tall. Each rosette is green in the center and dark burgundy moving outward. Unlike sempervivums, leaf color remains year-round. The plants are excellent on rooftops and in rock gardens. They do best in fast-draining soil in areas that get full sun. Give them some shade in hot inland areas. Hardy to 30°F.

KALANCHOE

I SEE A LOT OF SIMILARITY of form among echeverias and aeoniums. But take a close look at the kalanchoes, and you will discover how wonderfully diverse this group can be, some with sprawling stems and leaves covered in powder, others growing tall with big fuzzy leaves. Most are hardy to 32°F.

Many kalanchoes produce showy flowers in a broad array of colors from bright reds, oranges, and yellows to softer lavenders and whites. While a few, like *K. beharensis*, will not bloom until 6 or 8 years old, most produce flowers each year after they are 1 to 2 years old.

K. blossfeldiana

These tough little beauties are sold at supermarkets in an endless array of flower colors and can be found in homes all over the world, thanks to nearly endless introductions from hybridizers. This species branches to create a small, tight bush 4 to 6 inches tall. Leaves are smaller than those of the hybrids. They start out green, turning reddish in winter. Dark red flowers appear in spring. These plants are good choices for both landscapes and containers.

K. beharensis

Large velvety leaves, each 6 to 8 inches across and 15 to 20 inches long, inspired this plant's best-known common name: felt plant. Leaves are covered with fine hairs that are creamy greenish white, turning to brown with maturity. Older leaves drop off the stems, leaving beautiful markings where the leaves separated. Stems grow 2 to 3 inches in diameter, branch out, then wander as they reach as tall as 6 to 10 feet. The plant makes a very attractive specimen both in containers and in the landscape.

K. fedtschenkoi 'Variegata'

This upright shrub, 2 to 3 feet tall and 15 to 20 inches wide, branches freely. Some leaves are creamy white, some light blue, some a mix of the two, and all are infused, at times, with pink. The plant is also available with leaves of light bluish gray. Salmon-colored, bell-shaped flowers bloom in spring.

K. luciae

Paddle-shaped leaves have earned this lovely succulent its common name, paddle plant. It thrives in containers and grows well in landscapes that are warm and dry. (In cold, damp areas, like my coastal home, it does not do well, unless located in the warmest, most protected spot in the garden.) In late winter to early spring, it produces a large powdery inflorescence, with light yellow flowers, that needs to be pruned as the flowers fade, so the plant can put energy back into growing new leaves.

K. marmorata

This showy, branching shrub grows 12 to 15 inches tall and 15 to 20 inches wide. Large leaves, each 3 to 5 inches long and 2 inches wide, are a blend of creamy yellow and slight green, with striking purple splotches on the surface. They are borne on ½-inch-thick stems. Long white tubular flowers appear on 15-to-20-inch-tall stems in spring.

K. orgyalis

This upright, medium-size shrub has very distinctive spoon-shaped leaves, hence its common name, copper spoons. It branches freely as it grows, to 6 feet tall and 2 to 3 feet wide. Leaves, 3 to 5 inches long and 2 to 3 inches wide, are covered with velvet that's rich brown on the top, creamy brown on the underside. Yellow flowers appear in winter.

K. pumila

Whether spilling from hanging baskets or cascading gracefully over a garden wall, this low groundcover is a stunner. Narrow, 1-inch-long leaves on thin ⅛-inch stems look powder coated, almost snow-white, accented in spring with purple flowers. For a fuller look, prune stems of young plants to force branching.

MESEMBRYANTHEMUM

KNOWN FOR THEIR bright dandelion-like flowers that close when the sun disappears behind clouds or as evening arrives, *Mesembryanthemum* are South African natives. Some varieties make excellent, rapidly growing groundcovers. Others are small, low, clumping types favored for use in rock gardens, rooftop plantings, and miniature fairy gardens. After several years, groundcover types develop a thick woody thatch under the new foliage; they look their best if replanted every 6 to 10 years. Pests and disease are seldom a problem if plantings are well maintained. Most of these plants grow during the fall, spring, and mild winters, followed by a rest period in summer. During growth periods, increase watering and feeding to step up the growth rate. Most are hardy to 28°F.

Oscularia deltoides

This red-stemmed groundcover forms a mound 3 to 5 feet across and 1 to 1½ feet tall. It cascades nicely over walls. Small, silver-gray leaves give it a unique texture. Lavender flowers are dazzling in the spring. The plant is hardy to 28°F, but I have seen it regrow after temperatures of 19°F cause it to die back.

Othonna capensis

This moderately slow-growing ground-cover from South Africa forms a dense clump to 3 inches tall and spreads 1 to 3 feet wide. Fat, dark green leaves about 1 foot wide are pickle-shaped and give the plant its common name, little pickles. Yellow daisy flowers appear sporadically spring through fall, sometimes flowering nonstop. The plant is attractive in hanging baskets. It is subject to rot if it gets too much water in winter, especially when sunlight is minimal and airflow is limited. Hardy to 10°F.

Plectranthus tomentosa

One of my favorite companions for succulents, this succulent-like perennial has fuzzy, lime green leaves that give off a minty-lemony scent when touched. Stems grow 10 to 15 inches tall and make a handsome shrub. Purple flowers appear in spring and fall. Some say it has medical benefits on the par of *Aloe vera*. Hardy to 28°F.

PORTULACARIA AFRA

FOR MANY YEARS, *P. afra* and *P. afra* 'Variegata' were the only varieties available at nurseries. Now, you can find others that are well worth exploring. All are sure to prove their worth in water-wise gardens. The plant performs well in a wide range of environments, full sun to partial shade, in containers and in the ground, and thrives in coastal and inland areas. It is seldom troubled by pests, although aphids might occasionally appear on new growth, and mealybugs on unhealthy plants. Flowers are somewhat of a rarity, so the foliage and growth habit are the focus. The plant is hardy to 25°F.

P. afra grows upright to 6 to 8 feet or more. Shiny emerald green leaves are tiny, ½ inch across, on red stems 1 to 2 inches thick. The plant branches heavily, creating a thick, tightly woven bush 3 to 4 feet across; it makes an excellent privacy hedge. 'Prostrate Form' (shown below) has the same green leaves, slightly smaller, but grows just 6 to 12 inches above the ground. 'Variegata' (shown on page 184) remains low over the ground, perhaps 1 foot tall. Leaves with whitish yellow and green variegation emerge from red stems.

TIP

Portulacaria is easy to shape and train, making it perfect for beginners who want to try bonsai. Plant it in an attractive bonsai container, and then prune it to form a mini tree.

S. dasyphyllum

This Mediterranean native forms a low mat of densely packed, gray-green leaves. It prefers partial shade. Among the many variations, most of which are probably naturally occurring hybrids, I particularly like these three: *S. d.* 'Fuzzy Wuzzy' (shown at left), *S. d.* 'Minor', and *S. d.* 'Major'. All have light blue foliage, though they vary in texture. From a distance, they make attractive groundcovers. But for me, the magic happens when I can view them up close—in spaces between rocks and stepping-stones, for example—where they nest so well. I especially like planting them between granite stones, since their light blue leaves appear to bring out the silver flakes in the granite. Leaves of both *S. d.* 'Minor' and *S. d.* 'Major' turn pinkish blue with age. White flowers appear in summer.

SEDUM

THESE PLANTS MAY LOOK DAINTY, but they are very tough, hardy, and easy to work with. They come in a wide array of colors and textures, and lend themselves to a range of gardening projects. When I look at sedums, I imagine them nestled in crevices between rocks or covering the soil where they complement the plants growing around them. There are so many ways to use them...just imagine!

One of the best uses for sedums is to replace thirsty lawn with them. Many are colorful, low-growing, and as richly textured as magic carpets. Don't walk on them, though as I have heard some people suggest; sedums simply cannot stand up to foot traffic. Plants that are crushed or bruised are more susceptible to pests and diseases. Instead, put down a steppingstone path so you can travel through the planting with the least amount of damage. As the plants grow, they will nestle nicely among the stones and visually soften the paver edges.

I like the way water beads up like jewels atop the tiny leaves, and I look forward to morning strolls through my garden when the dew has collected and the beads sparkle in the sunlight.

As new flowers appear, often in summer, check the new leaves periodically for aphids. Also watch for snails, especially on deciduous types that are trying to push out new growth in spring. Most of these plants are quite hardy—to 20°F or 25°F and some even to 0°F—and produce some of their best color during cold spells. I like to plan for a particular plant's winter color by placing a rock nearby to help it stand out as the color intensifies. All take full sun, except where noted.

Many choice sedums work well in rock gardens, in containers, and more. Some make attractive shrubs.

S. dendroideum

This attractive plant grows 2 to 4 feet tall, forming a nicely mounded shrub 3 to 5 feet across. Foliage changes from light green to bright red in the winter when in full sun. Bright yellow flowers appear in spring and contrast beautifully with the red leaves.

S. 'Fine Gold Leaf'

This plant forms a dense mat of yellow-green to lime green foliage that is so striking you can see it from a distance. Growing only 2 to 3 inches tall and spreading up to 12 inches, it nests beautifully between rocks and pavers. Flowers are insignificant, small and pale yellow. Protect it from hot sun and frost.

S. makinoi 'Ogon'

This low groundcover has striking yellow-green leaves, making it a favorite of mine for use in partly shaded gardens. It thrives in semishade, and cascades over walls or boulders, and nestles between rocks. Yellow flowers appear in summer.

S. hispanicum

The very dense, carpetlike growth is similar to that of S. dasyphyllum. My favorite is S. h. 'Purpureum', because its foliage colors are so beautiful; the bluish gray leaves take on a purple cast in direct sun, where they complement the light pink, star-shaped flowers that bloom in summer. Good drainage is a must to prevent stems from rotting under the dense foliage.

S. nussbaumerianum

This plant forms a beautifully dense mound 2 to 3 feet across and 1 foot tall. Narrow, thick, 1-to-2-inch-long leaves are similar to those of Graptoveria or Graptopetalum. Stems just ½ inch thick grow 1 to 1½ feet long, creeping along the ground or cascading over retaining walls or the side of a container. White flowers appear in summer or fall.

S. oxypetalum

Commonly called dwarf tree stonecrop, this sedum forms a dwarf tree, 3 to 5 feet tall. Sometimes deciduous, it changes character throughout the year—sending up pretty, white, star-shaped flowers in late summer, then dropping its leaves in fall. It remains leafless through winter, when it reveals more clearly the very attractive stout trunk covered with thin papery bark. I like to use this sedum as a bonsai plant in an attractive container, or in a rock garden.

S. pachyclados

A distinctively textured groundcover, 2 to 3 inches tall, this plant spreads 6 to 10 inches in a season. Little rosettes on this dusty blue-green stonecrop have a lacy look, due to the serrated leaf tips. Yellow flowers appear in summer.

S. pachyphyllum

This ground-hugging succulent has leaves resembling little green jellybeans. The plant grows 10 to 12 inches tall, spreading 6 to 12 inches across in a season. The pastel green leaves develop attractive red tips in full sun. Yellow flowers bloom in summer.

TIP

Use the smallest sedums in pots, dish gardens, or miniature gardens; larger types in beds and borders. Most are easy to propagate from stem cuttings.

S. rupestre 'Angelina'

Similar to *S. r.* 'Blue Spruce', this evergreen, mat-forming plant grows 6 inches tall or less, and spreads to about 2 feet. Leaves are yellow in full sun, chartreuse with some shade; in cold-winter climates, they turn reddish orange in fall. Star-shaped yellow flowers appear in summer.

S. × *rubrotinctum*

Commonly called pork and beans, this plant has sprawling, leaning stems set with leaves shaped like small beans. They are shiny and green, turning bright red in winter—hence the plant's second common name, Christmas cheer. It grows 6 to 12 inches tall and spreads 10 to 12 inches in a season. Yellow flowers appear in summer. *S. r.* 'Aurora' is attractive and has slightly opaque whitish leaves that turn hot pink toward fall and in winter. It does not respond well to pruning.

S. rupestre 'Blue Spruce'

Forming a dense mat 6 to 8 inches tall, this sedum grows 6 to 12 inches across in a season. Conifer-like foliage of dusty light green to blue gives the plant its rich texture. It is useful in rock walls, on green roofs, in containers, and along garden paths. Yellow flowers appear in summer.

S. spathulifolium

S. s. 'Cape Blanco' (shown at right), a low, creeping groundcover, 1 to 2 inches tall, spreads 6 to 8 inches in a season. Small leaves are powdery white. Yellow flowers appear in midsummer. Very drought-tolerant, it is good in rock gardens. *S. s.* 'Purpureum' (shown on page 184) is similar in habit to *S. s.* 'Cape Blanco', but with deep burgundy-purple leaves. I like to plant it en masse next to a swath of 'Cape Blanco' for the beautiful contrast they make.

SEMPERVIVUM

LIKE *ECHEVERIA ELEGANS*, sempervivums are commonly called hens and chicks because the mother plant, or hen, surrounds herself with new plants, the chicks, resulting in a cluster that expands annually. I always look forward to the appearance of new batches of chicks, generally in spring and early summer. I can remove some of the chicks to plant in my vertical gardens.

TIP
Small, shallow-rooted sempervivums are perfect for living pictures. Mix several varieties together and watch how beautifully they'll weave a colorful tapestry.

These evergreen plants from northern Europe are known for their tightly packed, generally small rosettes. They stay low to the ground, 2 to 3 inches tall and possibly a little taller when cramped quarters cause them to mound. Don't let their size fool you, though: They are tough plants that can stand up to temperatures well below freezing. They thrive in cool, damp climates like the Pacific Northwest but struggle in hot, dry conditions, making them unlikely candidates as houseplants.

Shallow-rooted, they are ideally suited to containers, and they make excellent candidates for vertical gardens. And because they come in so many leaf colors and textures, you could craft a richly diverse wall picture using only sempervivums! (They've remained my go-to plants for vertical gardens since the 1970s.) Plus, the leaves can change color radically through the year. Red, purple, burgundy—all the darker colors, basically—tend to intensify in fall and winter and fade toward summer.

Flowers appear randomly in the summer and are usually white, lavender, burgundy, pink, or some combination. A plant will die after it flowers, and the remaining plants will take its place.

Sempervivums are ideal candidates for planting between rocks, especially in a retaining wall; as new chicks push out of the cracks, they look for crevasses to latch onto and, once established, will grow. They are easy to use when planting wall pictures, because cuttings are simple to root and fill in uniformly when planted leaf tip to leaf tip for a full look.

Pests and disease are seldom a serious problem for healthy plants. But aphids go after the new leaves, particularly in the early to late spring, and at times will attack flowers. Mealybugs are the most persistent pests, both on the foliage and in the soil. If allowed, snails chew on the leaves. Sempervivums prefer full sun. All are quite hardy, handling temperatures of 10°F and below.

S. arachnoideum

Commonly called cobweb, this rosette grows ½ to 1 inch across. Looking closely at it, you could swear that a spider has been at work. The denser the cobweb growth, the whiter the plant appears. Leaves are dark green, but are hidden behind the webs. There are many larger hybrids, all with intricate cobweb patterns. I love to use this plant in vertical gardens to provide strong contrast.

S. 'Black Rose'

This open-growing rosette grows to 3 inches in diameter. It shows strong burgundy colors in winter, bright green in summer.

S. calcareum

This plant is one of my favorites because of the distinctly colored rosettes, 3 to 4 inches wide, which have bluish green leaves tipped in burgundy. The leaves never fade.

S. 'Commander Hay'

This variety forms one of the larger rosettes of the group, 6 to 8 inches in diameter. Foliage varies from dark burgundy to gray-green, sometimes mottled with a mix of these colors.

S. 'Dea'

Rosettes are 2 to 4 inches in diameter, green in the center and light burgundy toward the tips. The plant is fully green in the summer and as a juvenile.

S. 'Emerald Rose'

Rosettes grow 2 to 3 inches across, producing semisoft leaves that are light green.

S. 'Green Wheel'

Tiny, tightly packed rosettes, 1 to 2 inches across, maintain their bright green color. Use this little beauty beside burgundy-leafed varieties for contrast in succulent pictures. It also grows beautifully in rock crevices.

S. 'Director Jacobs'

This flat-faced rosette is 4 to 5 inches across and has green leaves infused with burgundy that is more intense in winter than in summer.

S. 'Hopewell'

Open-faced rosettes, 3 to 4 inches across, have leaves that are broader toward the tip. A burgundy blush on the leaves comes and goes with the seasons.

TIP

Sempervivum produce offsets in spring that will mature within 2 to 3 months. Remove them and plant in a container.

S. 'Jungle Shadows'

Rosettes grow to 4 or 5 inches in a nice open habit. Leaf colors are variable, from fully burgundy to bronzy green.

S. 'Kalinda'

Growing to 3 inches in diameter, rosettes consist of tightly packed leaves of bluish green in summer, developing a light purplish tip in winter.

S. 'Purple Fuzzy'

In this naturally occurring hybrid, the cobweb-like growth of S. arachnoideum is very apparent. Rosettes grow 2 to 3 inches across. The strong burgundy color remains year-round.

S. soboliferum

I like to use this naturally occurring hybrid in my vertical gardens, because it grows well in shallow containers and stays compact. A single plant produces 10 to 20 offsets in spring, so I refer to it as mother pupper. Unlike many sempervivums, the leaf color of this plant does not vary much through the year.

SENECIO

SOME ARE EXCELLENT GROUNDCOVERS, others sculptural shrubs. All are easy to grow in containers and in the ground. They will bring some wonderful textures into your garden, along with striking leaf colors that I find captivating.

For the most part, these plants are robust, relatively fast growers. When they get too large or are in areas where they are not wanted, take out the clippers and prune them 2 or 3 inches above the ground in spring and early fall. They take full sun in mild climates, partial shade in the desert. All senecios are sensitive to temperatures below 28°F. They are targets for hungry snails, and aphids are drawn to new flowers and tender young leaves.

TIP

Senecio serpens is a great groundcover; it grows just a foot tall and spreads 2 to 3 feet. Try it on a sunny hillside, or let it ramble around larger succulent rosettes in a garden bed.

S. crassissimus

Commonly called vertical-leafed senecio, this upright shrub, 1½ to 2 feet tall by 1½ feet wide, has thick stems and beautifully shaped leaves that are flat and pointy. Both stems and leaves are silvery gray with purple highlights. I love this as a stand-alone sculpture. It can be pruned to create a fuller look, but is quite attractive without pruning. Yellow daisy flowers appear in summer.

S. jacobsenii

Sometimes called trailing jade or Jacob's ladder, this creeping groundcover makes an excellent plant for hanging baskets. Thin stems grow 6 to 8 feet long. In shade, the leaves remain green, but even a little sun encourages them to turn a pastel pink. Dark orange flowers appear in winter. For a dramatic effect, set this plant in a tall container and allow it to cascade over the side.

S. mandraliscae

This fast-growing groundcover, 12 to 15 inches tall, spreads 2 to 3 feet in a year. I like mass plantings of this lovely trailer cascading down a hillside. I've also filled a wine barrel with cuttings that grew in beautifully and tumbled over the side, reaching the ground. Add a little shade, and the leaf color looks nearly neon blue. Tiny flowers are creamy white.

S. cylindricus

Formerly known as *S. vitalis,* this plant starts out as an upright shrub, growing 2 to 3 feet tall. Then it falls over from its own weight. Prune in spring to allow it to regain its appealing upright appearance. Pointy cylindrical leaves on tall stems sway nicely in a breeze. Creamy white flowers bloom in spring and summer.

S. serpens

Similar in color to *S. mandraliscae,* this plant is smaller and grows more slowly. Its shorter leaves give it a much different texture. I like to use it in rock gardens and between steppingstones. Flowers are white.

Now that you have found your design inspiration and discovered plants to try growing, you will want to know how to choose the best spot in your garden for them, and the best ways to plant and to care for them. On the following pages, you will find advice for selecting the healthiest plants at the nursery, and tips and tools to help you with soil prep, planting, watering, feeding, pruning, dividing, and grooming succulents—in containers and in the ground.

PLANTING AND CARE

GETTING STARTED

SUCCULENT PLANTS ARE EASY and fun to grow. They have a lot going for them, including fleshy leaves capable of holding water, which can help them withstand drought and protect them from fire. They thrive without much fuss on your part. Yet many gardeners, even some professionals, still find these plants a bit of a mystery to grow.

As with any other kind of plant, succulents need a little care to stay healthy and attractive. That starts with choosing the right soil mix and the best spot in your garden where they will not get too much or too little sunlight. Then you want to provide the amount of water they need and the right type of food in the right amounts. Pests and disease can occasionally attack some plants and need to be dealt with. Like many other plants, succulents have a seasonal rhythm—a time to grow and a time to rest. And they have maintenance needs to match, whether monthly, seasonally, or annually.

You need to feed succulents when they're growing, but not when they're resting or dormant. Growing times can vary. Aeoniums, for instance, grow in cool months and need to rest in warmer months. Echeverias, on the other hand, grow in warm months, then rest in colder months. Some sedums, such as *S. oxypetalum*, go fully dormant in winter.

Buy Healthy Plants

When shopping for succulents, choose healthy, pest-free plants. Check leaves for discoloration, breakage, or pitting, often a sign that pests have been chewing or sucking on the foliage. Examine flower stems on any blooming plants for signs of pests. Also make sure the plant seems well rooted in its container. A plant that wobbles in the pot may have a poorly developed root system, while roots protruding through the pot's drainage holes indicate the plant may be rootbound and need a bit more work loosening the roots before replanting.

At the very least, a plant should be labeled with its name, so you can look it up. Informative labels provide valuable information, including size at maturity, water requirements, cold tolerance, flower color, and bloom time, as well as the best exposure for the plant, be it sun or part shade.

Choose the Right Spot

When picking out the right succulents for your garden and the best spot to plant them, understanding your climate and your property's exposure to sun is essential. Coastal, desert, mountain, and inland areas each have their own climate characteristics. Some succulent plants grow in each, but not all plants are suitable for all these climates.

Flats of succulents create a patchwork quilt effect at Sierra Water Gardens nursery in Reno, Nevada, where many succulents are grown as annuals.

Chocolate-hued rosettes of *Aeonium atropurpureum* bask in the soft light and dappled shade of nearby bottle palms.

Moderate coastal climates favor the widest selection of succulents, including some that only do well near the California coast. Aeoniums, for example, thrive on the West coast, but struggle in the hot desert and freeze in the coldest high-mountain areas. That's because climates are more extreme in desert, mountain, and inland areas. While the selection of succulents sold at nurseries in colder, wetter, or hotter climates is limited, some great plants do well in these regions. These include sempervivums in the cold, damp Pacific Northwest, *Echeveria agavoides* in the hot inland areas of California, and the hardier agaves and *Dasylirion* in Colorado and elsewhere in the mountain states.

Track the Sun Where you place the succulents in the garden will affect how well they grow. Before you plant, watch how the sun moves across the garden for a few days, paying special attention to the bed where you want to plant.

Northern exposures are generally shady, which is perfect for plants such as *Aeonium atropurpureum* 'Variegata', *Aloe arborescens* 'Variegata', and other shade-loving succulents. Eastern exposures get direct sun in the morning and shade the rest of the day—prime conditions for growing some aeoniums, echeverias, and other succulents that appreciate soft sunlight.

Western exposures that get shade in the morning and afternoon sun are excellent for growing succulents such as *Aloe ferox* and *A.* 'Christmas Carol';

THE HARDY SUCCULENTS

Many succulents are quite hardy and can withstand temperatures down to 0°F or below. *Sedum spurium* is native to the Caucasus Mountains; *S. spathulifolium* is native from California's Coast Ranges and the Sierra Nevada north to British Columbia. Sempervivums are native to mountains of Europe and are therefore hardy. Try *S.* 'Kalinda', whose bluish green rosettes develop purplish tips in winter, or *S.* 'Jungle Shadows', whose purplish gray rosettes are flushed with burgundy in winter. All are beautiful rambling between boulders as shown above, in rock gardens, or carpeting slopes. Or display them in pieces of porous rock or in stone troughs. For a list of other hardy succulents, see page 184.

Echeveria agavoides 'Lipstick'; *Crassula* such as *C. capitella* 'Campfire'; and *Agave attenuata* 'Nova'. The slightly more intense afternoon sun will enhance the leaf colors of these varieties.

A southern exposure receives sun all day and works well for plants such as *Dasylirion* and most agaves, aloes, and echeverias, but is difficult for growing aeoniums and sempervivums. Trees can provide some shade for sunny areas, and if they're deciduous (dropping leaves in fall or winter), they'll offer more shade in the summer and less in the winter. Walls and fences can block sun or, when facing the sun, magnify its intensity.

Not all succulent plants thrive in hot sun all day, as many people think; most kinds perform well with just a few hours of moderately hot sun and prefer some protection from hot midday sun, especially in desert, inland, and mountain areas.

Your best bet when selecting an area to plant succulents is a spot that gets 3 hours or more of sunlight per day and has soil with excellent drainage.

SOIL

TO GROW HEALTHY SUCCULENTS, you need soil that is porous and provides good aeration; both are essential to developing healthy root systems. Unlike plants that do not store water in their leaves or stems and rely on soil that holds moisture to stay hydrated, many succulents come from areas where water is scarce, so they have developed the ability to collect, store, and use water efficiently. That's why they are susceptible to rotting in heavy soils that hold too much moisture.

Before planting, make sure your soil or potting mix is light and fast draining. Water should flow through it easily, allowing the soil to stay moist, not wet, for a little while. If your soil is too heavy, it will not drain well and will need amending to improve drainage.

Soil Essentials

Soil that is 6 inches deep is adequate for growing most succulents, but 12 inches of soil depth provides more space for roots to grow. Healthy root systems mean more robust plants that require less attention. To increase soil drainage and aeration, you can dig in crushed lava (⅛ inch to ¼ inch diameter). Or try coarse pumice (very similar to lava) or perlite. Given a choice of these three commonly used materials, I always go for pumice, because it supplies the most aeration.

White Pebble Blend

A mix of transparent and polished white nuggets, it's pretty in white pots around fuzzy-leafed plants such as *Kalanchoe tomentosa*.

⅜-inch Gold Granite

This is the mulch of choice for use in desert-style gardens and in succulent rockeries like the one pictured on page 109.

Polished Pebbles

Soft shades of gray help it pair well with sculptural plants such as *Aloe plicatilis* in contemporary white containers.

Black Bean Pebbles

A blend of small, polished stones in shades of black and charcoal to pale gray that's useful in charcoal-hued troughs and around *Dyckia* and similar "sea creature" succulents.

MULCHES

Eight of my favorite soil toppings for garden beds and container plantings

Tumbled Terra-Cotta

Chips come in various shapes and sizes, from creamy beige to nearly red. Use this mix to provide a rustic look to cactus in small garden beds and containers.

Wood Bean Pebbles

Varied shapes and shades from beige to caramel help this mulch add a natural touch around small cactus in rugged containers of the same hues.

Jade Bean Pebbles

Its small, smooth stones come in various shades of green; try it around blue-green echeverias in a low bowl glazed soft green.

Bahama Blend Glass Pebbles

Tumbled-glass pebbles in shades of aqua to deep sea blue look great in glazed pots of the same shades. For a tropical, lily pad effect in an aqua container, scatter it around *Aeonium tabuliforme*.

To amend the soil, you'll need to add a 1- to 2-inch layer of amendment on top of the bed for every 6 inches of soil depth you turn over, then mix it in thoroughly.

If the soil is too difficult to dig, build a simple raised bed on top by raking a 6-to-12-inch-deep layer of succulent planting mix into a mound. To contain the mound, place decorative rocks, bricks, or pavers around its perimeter.

**Mulch:
The Finishing
Touch**

Like icing on the cake, mulches (or toppings) cover the soil around plants to keep weeds down, help prevent moisture from evaporating too quickly, and give plantings a more finished look. Gravel, decomposed granite, decorative glass, and rocks, including 3- to 4-inch cobbles, are commonly used mulches around succulents. Some gardeners use ground bark chips. These are my least favorite mulch, because the soil beneath them tends to hold more moisture—not the best conditions for succulent roots.

For special effects, I like light green, 1-inch pebbles around *Senecio cylindricus*; dark blue sea glass under *Agave attenuata* 'Nova'; and ¾- to 2-inch California gold gravel under a mixed planting of succulents. All have a dramatic effect, making plants pop in the landscape!

To maintain a fresh look, I cover the soil with 1 to 3 inches of mulch, taking care to avoid piling it against plant stems, which can cause rot. If dust settles on the mulch (which happens during dry periods), I wash it with a light spritz of the hose to enhance the colors of the gravel or sea glass.

When you buy plants, buy your mulch to complement the succulents' foliage. It's decorating, after all.

SOIL AMENDMENTS

Mix any one of these into potting soil to improve drainage.

Pumice
A lightweight rock formed by molten volcanic material, it also contains trace elements such as phosphorus and iron.

Lava Rock
Porous and somewhat lightweight, it helps break up heavy soils. The best size for this purpose is about ½ inch.

Perlite
A lightweight, organic material.

PLANTING

SUCCULENTS ARE TOUGH AND FORGIVING. They store water in their thick, fleshy leaves and succulent stems, and therefore seldom wilt when the roots are disturbed. If you decide after planting that you don't like where you placed them, you can easily dig up and move them to another location.

If my soil is dry several days before planting, I water it with a sprinkler or by hand using a water wand so that it is easy to work by the time I'm ready to plant. Moist soil is much easier to dig and turn than dry or soggy soil.

Prep the Planting Bed

Before planting your succulents, turn the soil 6 to 12 inches deep—deeper if you wish—using a spade or shovel and a pick if the ground is still a bit hard. Next, add an amendment, such as coarse pumice or crushed lava if needed, and mix it thoroughly into the soil. Place any rocks, blocks, or bricks around your planting bed to retain the soil or to define the garden area. I like to set large decorative rocks or driftwood in beds as accents, nesting them into the soil 1 to 2 inches deep, then plant around them. Smooth the soil with a rake, adding contours if you like.

Play with Your Design

I place the plants, still in their nursery containers, in the planting bed where I think they'll look best. I start with taller, larger plants, especially those intended as main focal points, and set them where they show off best, yet will not hide smaller plants. Next, I place plants whose location is clear in my mind. This might be a group of plants that I will use to create a border alongside a pathway, or a single plant that I plan to add under one of the larger, taller ones.

Occasionally I'll step back to view the design from different points in the garden to make sure all the plants are properly positioned for best viewing from, say, a patio or living room window. I move some plants around as needed until I'm satisfied with the overall design. The rest of the plants—mostly smaller types like groundcovers, low rosettes, and low, clumping varieties—then fill out the remaining space.

Spacing between plants can vary, depending on the desired outcome. Succulents grow well and look good when they're crowded shoulder to shoulder, or with leaf tips touching, so overplanting is seldom a problem. Most clumping rosette types will fill a space in a year if planted on 12- to 15-inch centers. Groundcovers planted 1 to 1½ feet apart will fill in within 1 to 2 years. I adjust the spacing depending on the look I want both at planting time and down the road. Once satisfied with the overall design, I'm ready to plant.

FACE TIME

For best viewing, flat-topped rosettes, such as those of aeonium (pictured), need to face the path or patio from which they will be seen, so orient them when you plant them. This aeonium edges a path striped with grass and leans out from a low border. A leafy cover of low shrubs and perennials shields its thick-stemmed backside.

Plant

Start by planting the largest specimen, perhaps a 5-gallon *Aloe plicatilis*. Dig a hole slightly larger and deeper than the nursery container, then remove the plant from its pot. Plastic and flexible metal containers are easy to squeeze, which separates plant roots from container sides and helps the plant slide out more easily. If the plant is heavily rooted and difficult to remove, hold one hand over the soil, turn the plant upside down while holding the bottom of the container with the other hand, then tap the container edge against a post or wall and let gravity do the rest (catch the plant with the hand that is covering the soil). Loosen the roots on the sides and bottom of the soil mass so they can move into the new soil when planted. Check the roots for bugs before planting. If you find bugs, you will need to clean and treat the roots (see the Pests and Diseases section, page 270).

As you set the plant in its hole, be sure to orient the succulent to the direction you want it to face. Most succulents have an especially attractive side; it might be the silvery branches of *Aloe plicatilis* that look best from a certain angle, or the way an *Agave potatorum* 'Kichiokan' looks at the viewer when tilted. Always position succulents to face toward the front or viewing side of your bed. (Big aeoniums are examples: Their rosettes can tilt slightly upward, as though basking in the sun.) Some low-growing rosettes are more attractive when they're tilted toward the viewing area.

Set the plant into the hole with the roots slightly suspended above the bottom, holding it with one hand. Then, with the other hand, fill in with soil around the roots. The plant should sit slightly above soil level, as it will settle 1 or 2 inches after planting.

Special Situations

There are some unique planting situations where creativity is necessary.

Big spiny plants. When working with larger plants (5-gallon size and up), it's best to get someone to help you. But the planting process is basically the same. Plants such as agaves with vicious spines need special handling, like removing one-half to two-thirds of the lower leaves, so you can get closer to the plant without getting poked and for easier handling. The sap can be caustic, so wear gloves, a long-sleeve shirt, and goggles.

Tight spaces. Planting in narrow crevices or between pavers requires removing most of the soil in the crevice to make way for the plant's roots. Then shave the rootball to get it into the crevice, or between the paver. (Don't worry; the plant can take it.) When planting a rosette at the base of a rock, I like to dig under the rock with a hand trowel far enough to fit the roots in, making the plant look as if it grew out from under the rock. On plants with powdery leaves such as *Dudleya brittonii*, avoid removing any powder from leaves by holding the plants by the rootball.

Cuttings. If you're lucky enough to have succulent cuttings, you can plant them directly in the garden in mid-spring. Rosettes of echeveria and sempervivum are especially easy; just remove the cuttings or offsets from the mother plants (with about ¼ to 1 inch of stem), about 2 weeks before planting, enough time to heal (form scabs). Store them in a cool dry area out of direct sun during this time before planting. Some collectors like to heal their cuttings by gathering a few stems—say, of tiny echeveria rosettes—into small, dry vases for display indoors. Here they'll stay until their stems have callused or started showing some roots, indicating that they are ready to plant.

WATERING

SUCCULENTS ARE LOW MAINTENANCE, but not "no maintenance," as many gardeners might think. They collect, store, and use water efficiently, so they are able to withstand longer periods of drought than other plants, especially if they are mature, with well-developed roots. When the surf is up, I can grab my board, head to the beach, and ride the waves without guilt (my wife calls these surf sessions my "board meetings"). My plants won't complain if I miss watering them for several days or even a week. Most succulents look good with less than half the water that thirstier plants require, and they'll survive on far less.

There are no specific rules on when or how often to water, mainly because this is a diverse group of plants with differing needs. Watering is done seasonally when plants are actively growing, and most succulents fall into one of two categories: winter growers and summer growers. To better understand the watering of succulents, it is important to understand the needs of these two groups.

Cool-Season Growers

These plants begin growing—producing new leaves—in the fall. They slow down in midwinter and then resume growing through spring. They want to be watered weekly in containers and semiweekly to monthly in the ground throughout this cool-season period. As spring moves to summer and the weather heats up, particularly in more extreme climates, the growth slows to conserve water through the hot, dry summer. Aeoniums are winter growers; as summer approaches, they begin to shut down by dropping leaves. By midsummer—their period of rest, or dormancy—they will have no leaves, except at the tips of the remaining stems, so they do not need or want any water (they may even rot in wet soil). But do continue light watering in summer for plants that keep some leaves a bit longer, as aeoniums sometimes do in milder coastal areas. Other winter growers include European sedums, *Dudleya, Delosperma* and other ice plants *(Mesembryanthemum)*, and sempervivums.

Warm-Season Growers

These plants begin growing in spring and continue growing through summer and into fall. As spring progresses, they start to awaken and produce new leaves and offsets. During spring and summer, they want to be watered thoroughly and regularly—weekly in containers, semiweekly to monthly in the ground. *Crassula,* echeverias, kalanchoes, and senecios fall into this group.

I find that warm-season growers like a little water during the winter as well, especially if the plants are so dry then that the leaves are wilting. The

After spritzing
succulents, the
water beads up
on the leaves and
then shimmers
like jewels in
the sunlight.

best time of day to water them in winter is in the morning during clear weather; take special care to keep water off the foliage, where it can pool in leaf joints, and to water just enough to moisten the soil and the roots.

Agaves are exceptions to these warm- and cool-season descriptions. They do most of their growing during summer, but will continue to grow in the winter, as long as they receive water. Although they can survive long periods of drought, they will slow or even stop growing through dry periods.

No matter the category—warm or cool season or "anytime" grower—it is better to underwater than overwater. Remember to irrigate thoroughly during the growing season and sparingly—if at all—when plants are resting.

When and How Much to Water

Sometimes it's possible to tell if a plant needs water just by looking at it. Leaves on dehydrated plants shrivel as they dry out and look dull or, in the extreme, wrinkled. Well-watered plants, on the other hand, will have fat, shiny leaves. If in doubt, check the soil by digging down 2 to 6 inches with a trowel, or use a soil meter.

Young aloes have roots 6 to 12 inches deep; echeverias and sempervivums have shallow ones, 2 to 4 inches deep. When you water, irrigate slowly to wet the entire rootball. My rule of thumb: Water newly planted succulents slightly deeper than their roots, and established plants as deep as their roots go. As the plants grow and become established over the next year, their roots will grow deeper, and watering should also be deeper.

When fully developed, most succulents—including aeoniums, *Crassula*, echeverias, and sempervivums—have roots that reach 4 to 8 inches deep. Aloes and agaves have heavy roots that are 1 to 1½ feet deep, and sometimes deeper, within a couple of years. During the growing season, water these plants at least as deep as the roots reach.

Plants in containers need water more often than the same plants growing in the ground. That means weekly watering, because potted plants have less room for root systems. Container plantings in full sun will dry out faster than those in partial shade, and will need water more often.

Watering Tools and Techniques

Drip irrigation works well with most succulents, because it focuses water on the root zone. Overhead watering, whether by hand with a hose, with a watering can, or with a sprinkler, should be done gently, like soft rain. Nozzles for hoses and watering cans, and soft rain sprinklers are the best tools for this as they allow you to direct the flow beneath the leaves. Watering in the morning before the sun is hot is the best time, as it prevents water that lingers on leaves from heating up and burning the leaves.

No matter how you irrigate your plants, do so thoroughly and slowly so that the entire root zone is moist. Irrigate containers just enough that the excess water trickles out the bottom drain hole. During the winter months, turn off irrigation after the first rains, except in the driest of winters.

FEEDING

I PREFER TO USE LIQUID FERTILIZERS. But I avoid oily ones such as fish emulsion, primarily because any oily substance that gets spilled on leaves can remove any beautiful powdery coatings, resulting in less attractive plants. (If you can keep the fertilizer off leaves, fish emulsion works just fine.) I also avoid controlled-release fertilizers—those little beads or pellets that you mix into the soil—because they slowly release the fertilizer each time the plant is watered. I like greater control over when plants get fed!

Although some fertilizers are formulated specifically for succulents, it's not necessary to use them. Balanced, general-purpose fertilizers with an NPK of 10-10-10, or 20-12-12 (the percentage of nitrogen, phosphorus, and potassium as indicated on fertilizer labels) have worked just fine for my plants. As a general rule, I suggest cutting the recommended dosages by half, then feeding succulents only monthly during the growing season, especially when you want to encourage growth. As plants mature, I like to slow their growth by backing off on feeding and watering. As plant growth slows, form and color improve. For mature succulents—plants that have reached a size you're happy with—feeding every 2 to 3 months is plenty, whether they're in the ground or in containers. Reduced feeding is also a good way to harden off plants (toughen them up) before winter arrives. Plants that have been hardened off seem to handle colder temperatures better than plants that have been fed all the way into winter.

I always feed my plants through a fertilizer bottle that attaches to a garden hose. For smaller jobs, I just mix the fertilizer with water in a bucket.

Morning, while temperatures are still cool, is the best time to feed succulents; that way, the plants will have time to dry before nightfall. Many of the rosette-forming succulents, such as aeoniums and echeverias, collect water in their rosette centers, where new leaves form. But when chemicals, fertilizers, or pesticides are mixed with the water that collects in the rosettes, they can burn the leaves. After applying the fertilizer, a short burst of clean water from the hose or a spray bottle, directed at the rosettes' centers, will remove the chemical, but leave jewel-like beads of fresh water for you to enjoy.

Keep in mind that some plants—*Dudleya,* for instance—prefer less fertilizer than most other succulents, while *Delosperma* and other ice plants are heavy feeders that grow best with a full dose of fertilizer during the cool-season growing period. So do deciduous varieties as they are coming out of dormancy.

MAINTENANCE AND GROOMING

ESTABLISHED SUCCULENTS ARE PRETTY CAREFREE. Still, there are times when you need to take steps to keep them looking and growing their best. Perhaps your agave has grown too large for its spot in the garden, and you need to move it to a roomier bed. Or maybe your echeverias have grown rangy, with rosettes clinging to the ends of long, skinny stems, and you need to cut them back. Maybe some succulent flower stems have dried and need removing. Here's how to tackle these essential chores.

Moving and Transplanting

Because most succulents have shallow roots, they are easy to dig and move, and they suffer little during the process.

Use a trowel for small plants and a long-handled spade or shovel for larger plants. Dig up the plant with some roots and soil attached. I usually trim one-third of the roots with clippers, or the shovel if its edge is sharp, before relocating the plant to its new home. If the soil is moist, I wait a week and then water the plant thoroughly; if it's dry, I water thoroughly after planting.

To dig and transplant larger succulents such as beefy agaves, you need one or more helpers to lift, move, and hold the plant in place while filling the new planting hole. Protect yourself from caustic sap and spiny leaves by wearing long sleeves, pants, goggles, and thick leather gloves. Before digging and moving the big, spiny plant, use a sharp pruning saw to remove half to two-thirds of the lower leaves. This will help you get in closer for digging around the plant and also will make handling easier. Begin by cutting the lowest leaf, then work your way around the plant, cutting off each leaf 1 to 2 inches from the trunk. (This same process can be used every 2 to 3 years to remove older unattractive leaves and make way for new ones.)

With the lower leaves removed, you can now get close enough to dig a trench around the plant 1 to 2 feet out from the trunk and 1 to 1½ feet deep. Then begin digging under the plant from your trench. Periodically give the plant a push under the remaining leaves, and continue digging until the plant gives when you push it. Eventually you can rock it back and forth, then dig and move the plant.

Refreshing Succulent Beds

Some clumping aeoniums, aloes, and echeverias grow tall and rangy with age. When this happens, I dig up old plants and take cuttings from them to root, replant, and freshen the bed. I cut off rosettes, leaving 1 inch of stem, and store the cuttings in a cool, dry, shady area for 2 to 3 weeks, then plant them in nursery trays or pots filled with succulent mix. It takes 4 to 6 weeks for the cuttings to develop enough roots for planting back in the garden.

While the cuttings are rooting, I refresh the bed by pulling or digging out the remaining stems and roots of old plants (unwanted ones get tossed on the compost pile). I rework the soil, turning it over with a spade or shovel, 8 to 12 inches deep, then spread 1 to 2 inches of compost over the area and mix it in. Rake the area smooth, and it is ready for the newly rooted plants.

This method works well with overgrown clumps of *Graptopetalum*, *Graptoveria*, haworthia, and sempervivum.

Cleaning Succulents

During dry periods, I remove dust and debris using a hose nozzle with a gentle spray setting, in early morning while the air is cool, to direct water at each plant from a distance of 6 to 10 feet. A shop vac with a long nozzle can also remove leaves and twigs that have collected in succulent rosettes, and extra-long needle-nose pliers work well for reaching difficult areas to extract debris.

Tree aloes such as *A. plicatilis* tend to hold old, dry leaves below the newer ones, where they continue to cling to the branches for months and even years before falling off. I remove dried-up leaves several times during the year; they are easy to peel away from the branches by pulling them gently downward. I like the look of clean silvery branches with the fan shape of the newer green leaves at the branch tips. Using this same technique, I remove dried-up leaves from tall aeoniums, *Beaucarnea recurvata*, and *Dasylirion*.

All succulents bear flowers, and most bloom at a certain time of year. Aloes, for example, generally bloom in winter, while echeverias bloom in spring and summer. Agaves bloom only once, often not for 15 or 20 years, then die. As flowers fade and dry up, they will eventually fall away from plants on their own, but I remove them as they dry, to give the plant a cleaner look. Left in place, dead leaves can also attract insect pests.

When an aeonium blooms, the rosette at the end of a stem becomes a flower and then dies. I remove the entire flower stem by cutting it 1 to 2 inches from the bottom of the stem with sharp, fat, curved clippers.

Most agaves bloom only once, then die, leaving a dead plant and flower stalk to remove. If any offsets remain, they will grow in and replace the original plant. But it's best to remove and discard the dead agave, because it can take a long time, often years, to decay.

In summer, *Echeveria gibbiflora* hybrids produce large flower stems that pull energy from the plant, causing the plant to appear weak and unhealthy. When half of the flowers on a stem have faded, I remove the stem, which helps plant vigor. Sempervivum rosettes flower randomly, with only a few flowering rosettes at a time. After each rosette flowers, it will die. Remove dead ones to make room for surrounding rosettes to grow.

PRUNING

SUCCULENTS NEED PRUNING primarily to remove damaged leaves and branches, to reduce plant size, to encourage branching, or to thin overgrown plants. Another good reason to prune is to take cuttings for starting new plants.

The best time to prune your succulents is during the growing season for the varieties you grow. For best results, I fertilize my plants 4 or 5 days before pruning them. Cut upright branches at an angle so that water will run off the cuts, allowing the branches to dry out faster and resist rot.

Best Pruning Tools

I use narrow, pointed clippers to prune small sedums and *Crassula* and fat, curve-bladed clippers to cut thicker stems of succulents such as aeoniums, hybrid echeverias, and senecios. Paring knives with 3- to 4-inch blades work well for removing aloe leaves from stems. To cut fibrous agave leaves and thick stems, such as those on *Aeonium* 'Cyclops', a 10-inch serrated knife works best. For big agaves such as *A. ferox* and *A. americana*, I use a tree-pruning handsaw with a 12- to 18-inch blade. It also works well for thinning branches of *Aloe plicatilis* and other succulents with thick, fibrous stems.

Make sure all your pruning tools are clean and sharp, so they won't damage plant tissue or transmit disease from one plant to another as you prune. I like to clean my tools with disinfectant a day or two before pruning. And I wipe the blades with the disinfectant after I finish one plant, before going to the next.

Succulents that Benefit Most from Pruning

In my experience, most kinds will grow into very attractive plants with little pruning, except to remove old leaves and unwanted offsets. I seldom prune *Crassula*, echeverias, and sempervivums, for example. But I do remove older lower leaves from agaves and tree aloes at least annually, and I cut back senecios and *Calandrinia* annually for best appearance. I only cut back *Crassula*, *Cotyledon*, and *Portulacaria* to reduce or reshape them.

Below are my tips for pruning some commonly grown succulents.

Aeonium. Many grow quite shapely without pruning. In fact, *A. urbicum* and *A.* 'Sunburst' do not branch well after pruning. The main reason to prune these beautiful, rosette-forming plants is to take cuttings to use for starting new plants (offsets generally appear within 2 to 6 inches of the cut) or to shape overgrown plants.

Calandrinia grandiflora. Also known as *Cistanthe grandiflora*, this plant blooms from spring into summer. Hard pruning after flowering will encourage full branching and possibly another bloom period.

HOW TO PROPAGATE *ECHEVERIA*

A common characteristic of *Echeveria gibbiflora* hybrids, like the ones pictured below, is their tendency to grow upright. Unless you take steps to shorten them, over time their stalks will lengthen, losing their ability to transfer energy to the rosettes on top. The rosette (or head) will then shrink, and the lower leaves will drop off, leaving a bare lower trunk.

To encourage branching on the lower stalk, clip off the head, leaving 3 inches of stalk above the soil. The stalk often produces offsets (young plants, which are sometimes called "pups") in about 6 months, as shown below (middle).

The head that was removed (right) was planted in potting mix after 2 to 3 weeks of healing, then it produced new roots.

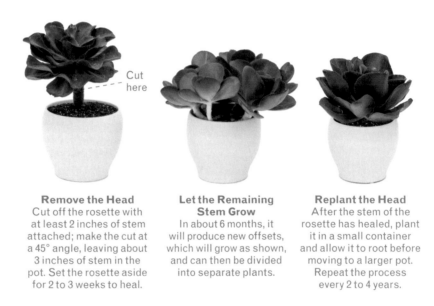

Remove the Head
Cut off the rosette with at least 2 inches of stem attached; make the cut at a 45° angle, leaving about 3 inches of stem in the pot. Set the rosette aside for 2 to 3 weeks to heal.

Let the Remaining Stem Grow
In about 6 months, it will produce new offsets, which will grow as shown, and can then be divided into separate plants.

Replant the Head
After the stem of the rosette has healed, plant it in a small container and allow it to root before moving to a larger pot. Repeat the process every 2 to 4 years.

Crassula. Jade plants and other *Crassula* will branch nicely without pruning. But light pruning can encourage fuller growth and shapelier plants. Cut overgrown plants almost to the ground and they will branch out well. Most other *Crassula* can be encouraged to fill out with pruning.

Echeveria gibbiflora. Hybrids of this species grow up on a stalk after a couple of years. If you allow a plant to continue to grow and elongate, it will flop over. You can remove the rosette at the end of the stalk every 3 or 4 years, in spring, then root it in a container filled with succulent mix, as shown above, before planting it in the ground. The remaining stalk may branch, but I remove it to make room in the planting bed for my freshly rooted rosette.

Euphorbia. Columnar types that have grown too tall can be pruned back to 3 to 6 inches above the soil; they will then branch nicely on the remaining trunk. Be careful to wear protective goggles, gloves, and clothing when pruning euphorbias, as the sap is poisonous. Wait for warm weather, June, July, or August, for best results, because these plants need heat to grow and form new branches.

Graptopetalum, Graptoveria. If overgrown, these plants can be pruned 3 to 6 inches above the soil, and they will send out new branches.

Kalanchoe. Prune to encourage fuller growth on most kinds of kalanchoe. (*K. beharensis,* commonly known as felt plant, or sometimes as elephant ear, is an exception; it does not respond well to pruning and usually won't form new branches after you thin out the old ones.) Remove broken or crossing branches, then prune back the remaining branches by several inches.

Portulacaria afra. This small-leafed jade plant look-alike can grow too tall or—in the case of prostrate forms—too wide. In both cases, the plants can be cut back to 3 to 6 inches above the soil level. They will branch from there.

Senecio. Thin upright types such as *Senecio cylindricus* and cut them back severely once a year in spring or late summer; make cuts 3 to 6 inches from the ground. Within 6 months, they will grow back nice and full.

DIVIDING

AT LA MIRADA, A HISTORIC OLD ADOBE BUILDING in Monterey, California, there's a beautiful border of *Echeveria elegans* planted between a pathway and a rose garden. At planting time, the rosettes were about 4 inches in diameter and spaced about 3 inches apart in garden beds. Each year they send out offsets and within 3 to 4 years become overcrowded. At this point, it is time for volunteers to gather, remove the plants, divide them, then plant back in the bed the ones needed for the garden to look as it did the last time the plants were installed. There are many more plants than needed for the replant, so a sale is held as a fundraiser to sell the extras.

As with these echeverias, many clumping succulents will grow crowded after several years, and need dividing and replanting. (Remember: Low maintenance does not mean no maintenance for these plants.) The benefits, of course, will be lots of extra plants that you can use to start

After the head
was removed
from this aeonium
stem, tiny offsets
started to form
near the cut.
Once their leaves
green up and
begin to unfurl a
bit, gently remove
them from the
cluster, set aside
for a few days to
allow the base (or
broken stem) to
heal, then plant
them in 2-inch
pots filled with
fresh cactus mix.

a new bed, to use in projects or give away as gifts, or even to toss on your compost pile.

When to Dig and Divide Succulents

Early fall is the most reliable time to dig and divide clumping aeoniums and *Sempervivum*, because they are just coming out of their rest period and will have 9 months of prime growing time to develop healthy roots, grow through winter, and then produce new branches and offsets the next spring. Sure, you can wait until spring to dig up and refresh your plants, but do your replanting as early in spring as possible to give the succulents as much growing time as possible before the summer dormant period.

Spring, on the other hand, is a great time to dig and divide aloes, *Dyckia*, echeverias, *Graptopetalum*, and *Graptoveria*, as these plants will have spring and summer to establish their roots and grow vigorously before slowing down for the winter. Fall will work for dividing these plants, but the transplants have less time to grow before their winter slowdown.

To divide clumping plants whose rosettes are attached to a single root system, gently pull the plants with their roots away from the main rootball. Plant any rosettes with some roots attached into the ground immediately. Plants without roots need to be rooted before being planted in the garden.

When you redo a succulent bed, keep in mind that you'll probably need fewer than half of the plants that you used for the original planting, and you'll end up with lots of leftovers. Difficult as it may be, you might need to toss some of these extras; otherwise, you could end up starting a nursery business, as I did. Or you could use the cuttings and offsets for making bouquets, terrariums, and more (for ideas, see the Easy Projects chapter). Or root them in containers to give as gifts.

A Word About Cuttings

When you take cuttings from clumping plants whose rosettes grow out on stems, be sure to leave 1 to 2 inches of stem on each rosette you remove. That way, you can root the cuttings in the ground or in containers. Once they are rooted, you can plant them elsewhere.

Even leaves can be used to start new plants; just insert healed ends into soil mix. This nicely rooted *Echeveria lilacina* is showing two tiny rosettes, indicating that it's ready to plant in a 2- or 4-inch pot.

Sunset aloe (*A. dorotheae*) suckers to form clumps of rosettes to 20 inches wide, and can overgrow the space where they're planted. When this happens, dig and divide them in spring.

PESTS AND DISEASES

THE BEST WAY TO KEEP PESTS and diseases at bay is to grow healthy plants. Pests and diseases are opportunists that always lurk somewhere, whether in leaf litter or in old potting sheds. But healthy plants have stronger defenses to protect them, just as healthy humans do.

One way to help ensure succulent health is to avoid overfeeding your plants. With succulents, a little fertilizer goes a long way, and what the plant does not use will remain in the soil, creating a fertile environment for pests. A half dose monthly should be plenty for any succulent. Also, keep plants clean, and dead leaves picked off.

If you spot an insect on your plant, take steps to banish it before its population grows. If you can't identify the pest that's feeding on your plant, take a sample in a plastic bag to a nursery professional, master gardener, or agricultural extension service for identification and treatment options.

The pests that I have found most troublesome on succulents are described below.

Common Succulent Pests

Ants. Most ants do not suck plant juices, but some species protect sap-sucking insects such as aphids and mealybugs for the honeydew they produce. Put sticky barriers around plants, or use insecticide baits.

Aphids. These tiny, soft-bodied, green or black bugs appear on flowers and new leaves—indoors or outdoors. They suck plant juices and remove sap, causing discolored, wilted, or stunted growth. They're easy to remove with a blast of water from the hose. If that fails, remove and discard the affected flowers or leaves.

Caterpillars. Moths lay eggs that produce caterpillars, which can chew leaves or burrow inside a succulent's main stem. The trick is to catch the caterpillar before it burrows. You can handpick it, especially at dusk, or spray with *Bacillus thuringiensis (Bt)*.

Gophers. These furry soil dwellers love agave roots and have destroyed some really big plants by eating their way up the roots and into the heart of the plants above the soil. If you live where gophers are troublesome, such as near wildland, use gopher baskets or traps. Gophers also burrow under other succulents, but seldom eat them.

Mealybugs. These little oval bugs have overlapping plates with a cottony white covering. On plants, they resemble tiny bits of cotton, most often on leaf undersides, or they nestle between leaves and concentrate in new growth. (Don't confuse their cottony white coating with the natural, powdery white coating on succulents such as *Dudleya brittonii*, as some of my customers have.) Mealybugs are very persistent, so you have to be even more persistent to get rid of them.

If infestations are light, try dipping a cotton swab in rubbing alcohol, then dabbing the insects (it kills them) and tossing the swab. For heavier infestations where mealybugs have established themselves in the soil, as well as on the leaves, you'll need to remove the plant from the soil, wash the roots thoroughly, air-dry them, then replant in clean soil in the ground or a container. For more persistent pest infestations, consult a nursery professional, a master gardener, or a local Cooperative Extension Office about treatment options.

Snails and earwigs. Succulents with small patches chewed out of their leaves are usually being visited at night by snails or earwigs (both dine on plant tissue). Like me, snails are attracted to beer, so some gardeners leave cups of beer around plants, which invites the snails to drink and drown. (Unlike me, they will drink any cheap beer!) Earwigs like to hide in dark confined spaces, especially during the day. Try setting out traps of rolled newspaper, corrugated cardboard, or pieces of an old hose for them to hang out in, then dispose of them in soapy water or sealed plastic bags.

Diseases

Botrytis and powdery mildew, which are both fungal diseases, sometimes attack succulents. Mildew can appear on leaf surfaces, usually in humid environments such as greenhouses. Botrytis grows on water drops between leaves, especially on echeverias and mostly in winter months; if the leaves are discoloring and turning to mush, there's a good chance botrytis is present. You can keep these diseases from your plants by providing good airflow and using good watering practices. Nurseries sell fungicides for treating each of these diseases.

Black aphids pepper this echeveria bloom stalk. If you spot them on your plant, blast them off with a jet of water from a hose.

WEATHER PROTECTION

I'VE ALWAYS BEEN FASCINATED by differences in weather throughout the year. Big thunderheads producing lightning and hail in the spring, long summers without rain May through October, and walking through icy puddles all played an important part of my life growing up. Those same weather extremes—from hot sun to flooding rains (except during droughts)—can have harmful effects on the succulents you grow, unless you take steps to protect your plants.

Wind

High winds can cause the tall stems of aeoniums to snap, unless you support them with sturdy stakes. Tall, shallow-rooted plants such as *Euphorbia ingens* may blow over, but can be supported by staking or by placing a couple of attractive rocks around the base. Damage to long, thin leaves can be avoided by locating plants in a protected area, such as along a wind-blocking fence or wall.

Sun

Hot sun will burn plants that get moved outdoors too quickly from a sheltered indoor space, such as a greenhouse or a bright living room window, unless you take protective measures. After bringing the plants outdoors, cover them with a piece of shade cloth for a week or two. Then remove the cloth in the evening or on a cloudy day, giving plants time to harden off (toughen up) so that they are better able to tolerate outdoor conditions.

Edema in succulents, mostly agaves and aloes, is a condition that manifests itself as sores on leaf surfaces, followed by scabbing. It happens most often when a plant growing in wet soil is left inside a warm, dark room or vehicle for several hours. (Crack open windows for better air circulation when transporting succulents in your car on a hot day.) Certain weather phenomena—when clouds block or filter sunlight and combine with high humidity, limited air circulation, and high soil moisture—can also cause this condition. If this occurs, about all you can do is trim the affected leaves and wait for new ones to grow out.

Frost, Hail

In winter, cover outdoor plants with frost blankets or floating row covers, which can add 4°F to 8°F of cold protection. They are lightweight and allow plants to receive some sunlight. I've used these materials successfully for several years; when frost is predicted, I just cover sensitive plants by draping the blanket over stakes placed around them, with the blanket raised slightly above the leaves. (Or you could build frames of wood or PVC pipe to hold the cloth above the plants, as pictured opposite.) For extra heat, try adding a strand of outdoor Christmas tree lights beneath the cover, arranging them where they will not touch the fabric.

Protect tender succulents such as *Aeonium* 'Sunburst' from frost and hail by covering the plant with a frost blanket. Don't allow it to touch the succulent foliage; instead, lift the blanket on stakes, or make a removable frame such as shown here.

DORMANT SEASON CARE

GROWING HEALTHY SUCCULENTS requires an understanding of seasonal cycles—the periods when the plants grow and when they rest. Most of my succulents do much of their growing in fall and spring and then stop growing in summer to rest. Or they go totally dormant, a more extreme form of resting, where the plant doesn't just slow or stop growing, but also drops some or all of its leaves. Deciduous sedums, for example, usually go dormant in summer or winter.

Many aeoniums grow actively during the cooler months of spring and fall. But in cool coastal climates, they will continue to grow through the summer rest period and well into winter, slowing down during midwinter and then again toward the end of summer. Where winters are colder and summers are hotter, these plants will stop growing to rest (with leaves still in place), before going dormant in summer, at which time they lose their leaves and only bare stems remain.

Deciduous succulents such as *Sedum oxypetalum* and *S. spectabile* go dormant in winter, particularly in locations where winter frost is common. *S. oxypetalum* flowers in late summer, then its leaves turn orange before dropping off, leaving bare branches. It remains dormant until spring, when it puts out new leaves, much like a deciduous tree. *S. spectabile* completely defoliates after blooming in late summer, then slips into winter dormancy. As daylight hours increase the following spring, the plant wakes up and begins pushing new stems out of the ground.

Some rest and dormant periods for various succulents are listed below.

Winter-dormant succulents. These plants include *Cotyledon, Crassula,* echeverias, euphorbias, *Graptopetalum,* kalanchoes, *Portulacaria,* sedums from Mexico, and senecios. In winter, I water resting plants lightly in the morning if the weather is clear, if the soil is dry, and if the plant's leaves are starting to wilt. A light watering should be just enough to penetrate the soil about 1 inch deep, which can rehydrate plants so their leaves will not burn or shrivel. I do not water plants that have defoliated (lost their leaves) and gone totally dormant.

Summer-dormant succulents. These include *Dudleya,* sedums from Europe, and sempervivums. I water these succulents lightly in summer, being careful not to soak the soil—again, just enough to hydrate the leaves without wetting the roots so much that they might rot in wet soil. I do not water dormant succulents such as aeoniums until fall, when they show new growth at the tops of their stems.

WINTER SHOW-OFFS

When many succulents are going dormant for the winter, others are just getting started. Certain aloes, for instance, send up spectacular blooms of vivid red or coral that can brighten the garden when all other plants are snoozing. Coral aloe *(A. striata)* puts out branched clusters of brilliant coral pink flowers from midwinter into spring. *A.* 'Super Red' sends up branched inflorescences of bright scarlet blooms in early winter. The aloe shown above, rising among shapely boulders at the San Diego Botanic Garden, shows off its tall candles of scarlet blooms in December. If you have room, add two or three of these aloes for pops of color in your winter garden.

Plant Needs During Dormancy

During their rest and dormant periods, succulents do not need water or fertilizer; in some cases, as with dormant aeoniums, the roots will even rot if the soil is wet.

Fully dormant aeoniums do not want to be watered. No matter what you do to encourage growth, they will remain dormant until the weather cools in late summer or early fall as daylight hours decrease. With a little fall rain, they start producing new leaves as they emerge from dormancy.

I don't try to take cuttings from succulents that are resting or dormant, because even the cuttings do not want to grow at this time, and it is difficult to get them to root.

After coming out of dormancy, plants that completely die back when going dormant, such as *Sedum spectabile* and *S. seiboldii*, like to be watered and fertilized more often than other succulents. Snails are fond of their new growth and will munch it all away if they are not controlled.

CONTAINER CARE

MOST SUCCULENTS ARE SHALLOW ROOTED and are easy to grow in containers, whether alone or with other plants. Containers have the advantage of mobility—you can display them practically anywhere, or move them to a protected spot during periods of excessive rain or cold, or even rotate the containers periodically for more even exposure to sunlight.

Keep in mind that plants growing in containers need more care than the same plants growing in the ground. That's because their roots are more confined in pots, resulting in a need for more watering and feeding. In my coastal garden, container plants thrive with thorough watering once per week. In hotter inland climates, potted succulents may need watering twice per week.

Best Container Materials

It is possible to grow succulents in any kind of container, including clay pots, plastic pots, abalone shells, plow disks, even old cowboy boots. Keep in mind that soil dries out faster in containers made of porous materials, such as wood or terra-cotta, than it does in containers that do not breathe—plastic, glazed ceramic, steel, and high-fired stoneware.

If I want to limit water use for a container planting, I opt for pots made of "no-breathe" materials. For hot inland areas, I wouldn't advise using steel containers, though, as they can get very hot in the sun and burn any roots that touch the pot's sides.

Bottom line: I choose containers mostly for the look I want, then modify my watering schedule to suit the container.

Container Size: Low Bowls or Deep Pots

Most succulents look their best in shallow containers, especially *Crassula*, echeverias, sedums, and sempervivums; all are low growers with shallow root systems that do not need deep soil. But taller-growing succulents, such as *Aeonium* 'Cyclops' and *Aloe speciosa*, look better in taller pots. Aloes and agaves have heavier root systems than other succulents and need larger containers for their roots to stay healthy.

When you plant succulents in decorative containers, think about the look you want. For a filled-in look, choose a container roughly the same size as the nursery pot your plant came in. But if you want the plant to continue to grow, choose a container that's at least 2 inches wider than the rootball of your newly purchased plant. In other words, go from a 4-inch nursery pot to a 6-inch decorative container, or a 6-inch nursery pot to an 8-inch decorative container.

After planting in the larger container, cover the soil with decorative gravel mulch for a more finished look.

Black containers, and a
short glass vase (front)
filled with black sand
and succulent "stones"
(Lithops), are ideal
choices for showing off
dramatic plants. The
square pot shows off a
nearly black *Dyckia*, and
especially this plant's
tiny, shark-like white
teeth. Black mondo
grass fringes the back
left pot; crested
euphorbias rise behind.

In a dish garden, plants can be set close together and even touch each other. If you want to allow a little space for them to grow larger, set them about 2 inches apart.

For easy care, the containers should have good drainage: Look for at least three drain holes in the pot's bottom. Or turn the pot upside down and use a drill with a masonry bit to add them.

Best Potting Mixes

Succulents need mixes that drain well and have good aeration; they should not contain high amounts of nutrients. The easiest solution is to buy a potting mix labeled "cactus" or "succulent" mix, which is already formulated for good drainage and aeration and the nutrition that succulents require. Most water-thirsty plants use more fertilizer than succulents do, so standard potting mixes are formulated to provide more nutrients; they're hotter and contain more fertilizer than succulents need.

Best Location for Containers

While succulents in containers do like some sun, placing them where they'll get too much sun increases their needs for water and fertilizer, and often results in plants that are stressed and less attractive, with burned or dried-up leaves. My best advice: Locate succulent containers where they'll get 2 to 4 hours of morning sun (my favorite exposure) or late-afternoon direct sun; either allows for good plant growth.

How and When to Repot

Repotting succulents is an important part of container care. And there are good reasons to refresh your potted plants when needed. First, potting mixes wear out in 2 to 3 years and should be changed out every few years. Dig up the plant(s), remove the soil from the roots and the container, clean the container, trim the roots a bit, then replant in fresh potting mix.

Second, a plant's slowdown in growth indicates that it might be rootbound, in which case I knock the plant out of its pot, trim the roots as needed, and move the overgrown plant into a larger container. Agaves and aloes need transplanting more often because they have much heavier roots than other succulents. When potbound, these plants slow their growth, and their leaves burn at the tips and shrivel.

Once your succulents have filled a container, you can either transplant them to larger containers or slow their growth by reducing feeding to one-fourth or even one-eighth dose monthly, and by watering only when the soil is dry. Or, if a plant has filled its container and you want it to continue to grow, it is time to transplant. As long as the plants look healthy, they can remain in the container indefinitely. When you repot your plants, don't forget to add fresh mulch or topping as well. Choose kinds to match your container (see details, page 253).

High Cylinder

Pot Size: 14 inches wide, 11½ inches deep.
Plant: Columnar plant such as
Euphorbia grandicornis.

Low Bowl

Pot Size: 15 inches wide, 5½ inches deep.
Plant: Center a single rosette inside,
or fill with small echeverias or sedums
from 2-inch pots.

Mid-Cylinder

Pot Size: 11¾ inches wide, 10 inches deep.
Plant: Columnar succulent, such as
Euphorbia mammillaris, or squat golden
barrel cactus, both from 1-gallon cans.

Lily Egg Pot

Pot Size: 15¾ inches wide, 14 inches deep.
Plant: Columnar type from a 2-gallon
pot, such as *Euphorbia ingens.*

CONTAINER AND PLANT PAIRINGS

—

**Here's a selection of
my favorite container styles,
along with ideas for
the kinds of plants to
grow in them.**

Paris Cache Pot—Large

Pot Size: 8½ inches wide,
7½ inches deep.
Plant: Small agave, aloe, or *Dudleya*
from an 8-inch nursery pot.

Paris Cache Pot—Medium

Pot Size: 7 inches wide,
6½ inches deep.
Plant: Upright aloe or a young *Crassula*
(from a 6-inch nursery pot),
such as *C. ovata* 'Hummel's Sunset'
or *C. tetragona.*

Paris Cache—Small

Pot Size: 5½ inches wide,
5¼ inches deep.
Plant: Any single, small succulent
from a 4-inch nursery pot, such
as a showy *Echeveria gibbiflora*
'Coral Glow'.

Low Rectangle

Pot Size: 3 inches wide, 5½ inches
long, 3 inches deep.
Plant: Single *Agave geminiflora* or
Haworthia fasciata 'Superbum' from a
4-inch nursery pot, centered, or three small
echeveria rosettes from 2-inch pots.

TIP
Arrange succulents
like artists use
paints: Blend beautiful
colors and shapes.

ACKNOWLEDGMENTS

Bernice Stockwell, my mother, who passed along whatever creative talent I have put to use with my palette of succulent plants.

Wayne Stockwell, my father, who loved tuberous begonias and showed me how passionate and sensitive a tough guy can be when it comes to plants.

Ron Michelson, owner of Half Moon Bay nursery, mentored me from 1963 to the present. No single person contributed as much toward my nursery experience. From the beginning, he answered my questions about soils, pests, watering, marketing, and retail, and always carried at his nursery the plants I grew. More than anything, he encouraged me to pursue the succulent experience.

Many people along the way, including retailers, growers, horticultural authors, landscape professionals, succulent enthusiasts, customers, suppliers, and great employees have contributed to my success—especially Tiffany Polli, a very special employee and friend. "It takes a village," the saying goes, and my village of support has been the horticultural community. No other group I know of is as down to earth.

I've had so much support while writing this book. The staff of Succulent Gardens—such an amazing group—and owners Megan and John Rodkin were extremely generous in providing plants and help with photo shoots. Brian Kemble, succulent hybridizer, landscape professional, and curator at the Ruth Bancroft Garden, has traveled the world to study succulent plants in habitat. He knows so much about these plants and has always been there to answer my succulent questions. The many talented landscape architects and designers, whose work is featured in this book, contributed great examples of succulents in gardens, and generously shared their experience with these plants.

The *Sunset* magazine staff; many have believed in me and in my mission to excite the world about succulent plants, and have worked with me through the years. I knew they all worked hard, but never realized just how hard until they, especially Kathleen Brenzel, pulled out the stops to help make this book a reality.

Wells Shoemaker, MD, who pushed me into places I never would have gone and showed me I could go further than I could ever have imagined.

Last, but not least, succulent plants, I love you.

Thank you all.
Robin Stockwell

Photography Credits

Caitlin Atkinson: 6, 44–45, 46, 47, 280–281; Aya Brackett: 279; Marion Brenner: 3 (Sunnylands Center and Gardens), 26–27, 108–109, 178, 284; Jennifer Cheung: 72–73, 88–89; Sophie de Lignerolles: 159; Caroline Greyshock: 102–103, 104, 105, 118, 120, 121, 122; Bret Gum: Front cover, 70–71, 80–81, 259; Steven Gunther: 124–125; Ive Haugeland: 18–19; Saxon Holt/PhotoBotanic: 273; Erin Kunkel: 63, 64, 65, 66, 67, 68, 69; Holly Lepere: 48–49; Amelia B. Lima: 90–91; Sara Shoemaker Lind: 14; David E. Perry: 17, 176–177, 275; Linda Lamb Peters: 10, 56–57, 106–107, 267, 283; Andrea Gómez Romero: 4, 130–131; Thomas J. Story: 13, 21, 24–25, 28–29, 30, 31, 32, 33, 36–37, 38, 39, 40, 41, 42–43, 58, 60, 61, 69, 74–75, 76–77, 78, 79, 82–83, 84, 85, 86, 87, 92–93, 94, 95, 96, 97, 98 (all), 99, 100–101, 116–117, 123, 127, 129, 132–147 (all), 151, 153, 164–165, 168–175 (all), 179–181 (all), 250, 253 (all, except top left), 269, 279 (all); Rebecca Sweet: 22–23, 34–35, 251; E. Spencer Toy: 2 (both), 148–149, 150 (all), 154–155, 156 (all), 157, 160, 161, 162 (all), 163, 166–167, 183–245 (all), 253 top left, 254 (all), 265 (all), 268, 271, back cover; Rachel Weill: 247, 249; Doreen L. Wynja: 50, 52, 53, 54, 55, 110–111, 112, 113, 114, 115, 256

INDEX

Measurement Equivalents

Refer to this chart for metric conversions. All equivalents are approximate.

⅛ in.	=				3 mm.		
¼ in.	=				6 mm.		
½ in.	=				13 mm.		
¾ in.	=				2 cm.		
⅞ in.	=				2.2 cm.		
1 in.	=				2.5 cm.		
1½ in.	=				3.8 cm.		
2 in.	=				5 cm.		
2½ in.	=				6.5 cm.		
3 in.	=				7.5 cm.		
4 in.	=				10 cm.		
5 in.	=				12.5 cm.		
6 in.	=	½ ft.	=		15 cm.		
7 in.	=				18 cm.		
8 in.	=				20.5 cm.		
9 in.	=				23 cm.		
10 in.	=				25.5 cm.		
11 in.	=				28 cm.		
12 in.	=	1 ft.	=		30.5 cm.		
24 in.	=	2 ft.	=		61 cm.		
36 in.	=	3 ft.	=	1 yd.	91 cm.		
40 in.	=	3⅓ ft.			101.5 cm.	=	1 m.
41 in.	=				104 cm.		
84 in.	=	7 ft.	=		213 cm.	=	2.1 m.
144 in.	=	12 ft.	=	4 yd	366 cm.	=	3.7 m.